WRITINGS ON BLACK WOMEN OF THE DIASPORA

CROSSCURRENTS IN AFRICAN AMERICAN HISTORY
VOLUME I
GARLAND REFERENCE LIBRARY OF THE HUMANITIES
VOLUME 2048

CROSSCURRENTS IN AFRICAN AMERICAN HISTORY
GRAHAM RUSSELL HODGES AND MARGARET WASHINGTON, *Series Editors*

WRITINGS ON BLACK WOMEN
OF THE DIASPORA
History, Language, and Identity
by Lean'tin L. Bracks

Writings on Black Women of the Diaspora
History, Language, and Identity

Lean'tin L. Bracks

Garland Publishing, Inc.
A member of the Taylor & Francis Group
New York and London
1998

Library of Congress Cataloging-in-Publication Data

Bracks, Lean'tin L.
    Writings on Black women of the diaspora : history, language, and
identity / by Lean'tin L. Bracks.
        p.   cm. — (Garland reference library of the humanities ; v. 2048.
Crosscurrents in African American history ; v. 1)
    Includes bibliographical references (p.   ) and index.
    ISBN 0-8153-2734-X (alk. paper)
    1. American fiction—Afro-American authors—History and criticism.
2. American fiction—Women authors—History and criticism.   3. Literature
and history—United States—History.   4. Women slaves—Biography—History and criticism.   5. Women and literature—United States—History.
6. Afro-American women in literature.   7. Group identity in literature.
8. Women, Black, in literature.   9. Women, Black—Language.   10. Slavery
in literature.   11. Prince, Mary. History of Mary Prince, a West Indian slave.
12. Marshall, Paule, 1929–   Praisesong for the widow. 13. Walker, Alice,
1944–   Color purple. 14. Morrison, Toni. Beloved.   I. Title.   II. Series:
Garland reference library of the humanities; vol. 2048.   III. Series: Garland
reference library of the humanities. Crosscurrents in African American
history ; v. 1.
PS374.N4B64   1998
813.009'9287'08996073—dc21
                                                                97-25403
                                                                CIP

The cover depicts "The Awakening of Ethiopia," by Meta Warrick Fuller. Bronze
cast (c. 1914). Photograph by Manu Sassooman. Schomburg Center for Research
in Black Culture (Art and Artifacts Division), The New York Public Library;
Astor, Lenox, and Tilden Foundations. Reproduced with permission.

Printed on acid-free, 250-year-life paper
Manufactured in the United States of America

Dedication

Giving honor to those who give life and help make dreams come true: God, my mother (Vivian), my son Bobby-Joe, the Bracks family and other relations. Special thanks to Dr. Maureen Honey and my friends and colleagues at the University of Nebraska at Lincoln.

CONTENTS

Series Editors' Foreword ix

Preface xi

Chapter 1 3
Literary Quilting: History, Language, and Identity
in Women's Diasporic Texts

Chapter 2 29
*The History of Mary Prince, A West Indian Slave, Related
by Herself*: History, Ancestry, and Identity

Chapter 3 55
Toni Morrison's *Beloved*: Evolving Identities from
Slavery to Freedom

Chapter 4 83
Alice Walker's *The Color Purple*: Racism, Sexism,
and Kinship in the Process of Self-Actualization

Chapter 5 105
Paule Marshall's *Praisesong for the Widow*:
Afro-Caribbean Rituals of Power, Place, and Identity

Bibliography 125
Index 135

Series Editors' Foreword

In the past thirty years, scholars in the field of African American studies have produced some of the most compelling and original books in American letters. Research on black leadership, labor, community, resistance, and intellectual tradition has blossomed into a field of inquiry of paramount importance. There has been a steady increase in historical scholarship, with younger academics reaching out in new directions and using innovative methodologies such as race and gender analysis. In works on all eras of American history, from each region of the country and even abroad, scholars today carry on the vigorous pursuit of knowledge and analytic interpretation that has always characterized African American studies.

Crosscurrents in African American History is a new series that aspires to publish the best and most recent research in the field. Garland Publishing is proud to present distinguished books that offer contemporary interpretations of the black experience in the United States. The topics in the series have been carefully chosen to fulfill this mission and to advance our knowledge of this critical field. Now and in the future, Garland will publish volumes that create new paradigms in African American historical scholarship, while resting securely on the accomplishments of established work in black studies.

Graham Russell Hodges
Margaret Washington

Preface

The study of literature can contribute to the understanding of the challenges of living that we all encounter and the interconnectedness of lives. Literary works thus offer a perspective to others that may spark, enlighten, challenge, or encourage different ways of interpreting experiences. My primary motivation for writing this book is to describe a model which may provide for today's black woman a means to take control of her destiny by retrieving her Afrocentric legacy from the obscured past. This model, I believe, can be found when we make ourselves aware of the history of black people, become sensitive to the complex interplay of written, spoken, and coded language systems, and remain appreciative of the extent to which black women writers must write against prevailing stereotypes of themselves. In this study I attempt to articulate the precise way in which a tripartite model of historical awareness, attention to linguistic pattern, and sensitivity to stereotypes in the dominant culture can illuminate texts by black women. Use of such a model can furnish us with guidelines for creating powerful identities in a world that tries to silence us.

I have selected the four texts for this volume (*The History of Mary Prince, A West Indian Slave, Related by Herself* [1831], *Beloved* [1988] by Toni Morrison, *The Color Purple* [1982] by Alice Walker, and *Praisesong for the Widow* [1984] by Paule Marshall) because they demonstrate in particularly striking ways the intense effect of an Afrocentric historical legacy on black women who have been abused, silenced, controlled, uprooted from their families, or lost in terms of a solid identity. The title character of *The History of Mary Prince* was an actual slave who suffered greatly at the hands of her oppressors; Sethe in *Beloved* is a fictionalized portrait of another slave woman, Margaret Garner, who killed her child rather than see her returned to slavery; Celie in *The Color Purple* is raped, beaten, and treated like a slave by her own stepfather and husband; and Avey Johnson in *Praisesong for the Widow*, a supposedly free woman, sacrifices her blackness to the American dream of success. In all four cases, however, we see these women drawing on hidden reservoirs of African legacies that enable them to develop a voice, a presence, and a proud persona that contradicts the destiny laid out for them.

Most importantly, it is the model that I offer to my readers, both female and male, as a means to secure the wealth of knowledge and layers of human complexity that exist in these texts and others. Many readers may miss the full extent of environment, struggle, and certain interplays of action and reaction because of not having a model to aid in accessing information. Without this model, alienation and misunderstanding could deflate the intensity of the middle-passage chapter that is recounted in *Beloved*, or one might accept the assumption that the term "ugly" actually describes Celie in *The Color Purple* and is not a response to the "image" society constructed of her as a black woman. Without it, readers might relegate Mary Prince to one who survived because of others' recognition of her human rights, and see Avey Johnson in *Praisesong* as a woman left with only a legacy of fanciful stories and folktales. By engaging this model readers will discover that Mary Prince understood and pushed the limits of her enslavement while claiming her human rights, and that the Ibo folktale taught to Avey was a lesson in taking charge of one's life even in the most hopeless of situations.

As a teacher and as a reader, I see this model as a means of peeling away at society-constructed stereotypes, and a continuation of liberating silences that unquestionably evoke emotion but must also offer learning to instill the lessons of survival—sometimes won, sometimes not. Hopefully this tripartite model will aid in allowing students of literary texts as well as the interested reader to see further into the intricacies of these works and offer a means to explore other texts.

WRITINGS ON BLACK WOMEN OF THE DIASPORA

CHAPTER 1

Literary Quilting

History, Language, and Identity in Women's Diasporic Texts

Literary quilting is a term I use to help conceptualize how history, language, and image/identity are important frameworks for understanding the way texts by women writers of the African diaspora can be stitched into our lives. Early on in my reading of the texts chosen for this study, I tried to describe how meaningful they were through the lenses of historical context, complexities in language use, and the development of an empowered identity for the protagonists that is specifically female and specifically black. The following words occurred to me:

> Speak to me in the language of my people so that I may hear and understand with my all-too-famous grin, while my heart sops up the truths. Those who hear and do not understand, know not who I am nor from where I have come.

I found myself no longer merely a spectator as I had been for the bulk of my reading experience, for when I contextualized this literature with a gendered Afrocentric framework, the stories came alive with meaning for today's black women who are in their communities living, loving, growing, changing, and seeking control of their circumstances in empowering ways. Those characters who evolve toward a greater sense of themselves in the four texts I have selected carry important messages for contemporary women of the diaspora and demonstrate that self-identity directly results from either honoring African-rooted ancestral legacies or ignoring them. I see a clear link among Toni Morrison, Alice Walker, Paule Marshall, and Mary Prince in that all draw on these African-rooted legacies for their strength, showing today's reader a path toward self-affirmation in a racist, sexist world that demeans, distorts, or minimizes black women's power.

Mary Prince begins this study because the dynamics of slavery in the Caribbean, which allowed for stronger cultural influences from Africa, enabled her to survive extreme powerlessness. She stands, therefore, as a stunning model of black female strength, and her narrative demonstrates the crucial role played by African legacies in creating that strength. Since women in many locations of the Caribbean during slavery were quite assertive in their verbal and legal protests against the subjugation of their race as well as being more directly connected with African traditions, Mary Prince's narrative gives us a female speaker who is keenly in touch with her own worth as a human being as well as examples of successful female resistance to oppression. Furthermore Mary Prince's voice, an important part of the historical record of our collective movement toward freedom, serves as an antecedent to black women who sought to define themselves in the nineteenth century while setting the tone for our subsequent passage to Emancipation, Reconstruction, and the modern era.

These points are well illustrated in *The History of Mary Prince, A West Indian Slave, Related by Herself* (1831), where we see a slave woman so strengthened by family and community that she voices her validity in the face of her captors' attempts to erase her. Mary's cultural and family influences, revealed through exploring Mary's personal history, redefine her out of the isolated position of a pitiful victim of slavery, bolstered by Christianization and the protection of her white supporters, into a woman who clearly recognizes that her own freedom is intricately tied to that of all slaves and that it is in her power to achieve it. The ability to see herself as part of a world free from subjugation was made possible by knowledge gained from newly arrived slaves, the availability of information about successful slave revolts such as that of Toussaint L'Ouverture in Santo Domingo, and the stories of women warriors who participated in revolts in the Caribbean as formidable fighters and tacticians. This historical perspective on Mary Prince's life makes it conceivable that she was a long-time participant in the fight for freedom before her narrative was presented.

Although much of her narrative obscures this rebellious context due to her deferential self-presentation, Mary Prince's assertiveness comes out clearly at various key points in the account of her growth from child to woman. We see a strong sense of her own agency develop, for instance, after she escapes a beating from her master by running to her parents' home, even though she is aware that the consequences of such defiance could be severe. Later on, she takes an even more remarkable stance when she stops her master from beating his own daughter as well as herself. These acts present us with a slave who is far from humble or intimidated or in need of rescue by a white benefactor. This narrative, when we examine it carefully as a record of the empowered development of Mary Prince, reveals an individual who was strong both in character and purpose and who well understood the limits of her own enslavement. It is true that our view of Mary Prince is somewhat flat and one-dimensional, but we should not let this obscure the clear agency behind her narrative strategy. Although Mary speaks passionately about her family, for instance, we learn little from her narrative about the writer as daughter, wife, and mother. This knowledge of Mary as an individual was silenced no doubt by her white publisher, Thomas Pringle, but we need to recognize that Mary did not want necessarily to reveal such personal information to a white audience. She had a much larger plan of freedom in her rhetoric that subsumed a statement of individual identity.

Although slave narratives were controlled by white publishers and abolitionists with their own agendas, texts like those of Mary Prince were effective vehicles for self-expression as we see in her case, but other forms of written history distorted more completely the viewpoint of black women. As W.E.B. Du Bois pointed out, the suppression of all but white-controlled accounts of history erased the perspectives of African American subjects and made recovery of black cultural memory crucial for balancing the record:

> in text-books, in popular culture, and in historiography itself, white supremacy in the present remained secure as long as historical memories were controlled or suppressed.[1]

Through the reclamation of Mary Prince's voice, we can better conceptualize the personification of Sethe, the focal character in *Beloved*, as a woman of courage and conviction who battles her way through the Reconstruction era and who emerges from Toni Morrison's quilting of Margaret Garner's story into historical memories of the black community. We can also, through reading Mary Prince, contextualize the struggles of Celie from Alice Walker's *The Color Purple* in seizing opportunities for empowering herself in the decades after Reconstruction. Alice Walker, like Morrison, fills some important gaps in African American history and addresses painful silences by bringing us to the early twentieth century when stereotypes of the black woman continued to devalue and misrepresent her worth. Paule Marshall in *Praisesong for the Widow*, finally, brings us full circle back to the Caribbean location that nurtured Mary Prince. She broadens the scope of cultural reclamation engaged in by Morrison and Walker as she moves from the United States to the island of Carriacou, Grenada, and metaphorically to mother Africa where all join together in a physical and emotional reclamation of the diasporic unity that can still exist. Marshall also moves us forward to the post-World War II period where we see the same issues of survival and identity for black women represented in the earlier eras. Avey Johnson, like the other protagonists discussed here, must step out from under a veil of invisibility in order to experience the freedom that is legally, but not psychologically, hers.

Although very different in setting, tone, time period, and narrative style, these texts share the central themes on which I focus in this study. Each looks to African roots for identity and power, for instance, whether the protagonist be legally enslaved or psychologically imprisoned. Each also deconstructs ongoing stereotypes of black women. Just as Mary Prince confronted and rejected the definition of herself as a slave, so do Sethe and Celie turn from images that dehumanize their acts of survival while Avey must turn away from internalized stereotypes of her race. Similar stereotypes were confronted in the characterizations of black middle-class females of earlier works by African American women who also sought to debunk these misconceptions, but I want to emphasize that these images continue to affect black women negatively despite the civil rights legislation and other advances that have been made in contemporary times. Morrison, Walker, and Marshall, no less than Mary Prince, must redefine what it means to be a black woman by focusing on a female protagonist who seeks to liberate herself from the baggage of stereotypes inherited from the past and evolve toward an identity rooted in African cultural influences.

All three contemporary writers focus on the key adjustments to Emancipation made by their grandmothers' generation, and I have chosen them in order to emphasize the ongoing importance of slavery's legacy of survival as well as pain to women writers of the diaspora today. History for them is not dead and buried but a living, palpable component of contemporary life which can be repressed, but at one's peril. African American writers of the past also brought the history of slavery into their imaginative landscapes, but today's narratives, in my view, are more psychologically complex and more consciously oriented toward a female perspective due to the previous literary generation's enormous obstacles.[2] Previous women writers had to break through serious barriers to their artistic expression, impediments that inhibited, to some extent, their full examination of slavery's impact on women.

A major impediment for previous women writers was the difficulty of finding historical perspectives other than those of white historians. The crucial recovery work by black and feminist scholars since the 1960s has provided today's writers the historical context they need to reconstruct an authentic Afrocentric framework for their characters. In effect, it became necessary to first free silenced voices of the present before the past could be effectively tackled. Then too, the blatantly racist stereotyping by the dominant culture viciously caricatured black vernacular and the rural or working-class population. To counter these stereotypes, most early writers such as Nella Larsen concentrated on the middle-class mulatto woman as protagonists. Although this generation could make the black female character focal, its treatment of race, class and gender was necessarily limited, and only a small portion of the black population was represented.[3] In addition, the black experience as a general rule in earlier texts was rendered so as to affect the white reading audience while conveying a more expanded sense of what it meant to be black in America. As necessary as this was for the removal of misconceptions regarding blacks, it did not fully address the deeper realities of black people's lives that affected their interaction with America and each other.

Today's writers are able to handle more comfortably and in greater depth characters who are neither middle class nor formally educated, and they are less concerned with reaching a white audience than with strengthening a black one. This altered social/political context allows black women writers to liberate the female voice by using colloquial dialect without so many of the problems faced by earlier writers such as Jessie Fauset or Zora Neale Hurston. Bolstered by a degree of social power unavailable to their early twentieth-century counterparts, Morrison, Walker, and Marshall can include vernacular speech without engaging in the debates which surrounded it earlier, primarily during the Harlem Renaissance. Furthermore, being able to focus on a black audience due to changes in the publishing industry, they can root their narratives more firmly in the political perspectives that benefit their characters.

Through a female protagonist who evolves from victim to self-defined agent, a complex narrative voice moving freely through the vernacular, and conscious retrieval of African cadences, then, the black contemporary woman writer seeks to make audible lost voices, both present and past. She further explores the pernicious legacy of slavery preserved within the historical memories of African American people while expanding what we retain about our African past. Quilting survival lessons passed on from Mary Prince to Sethe to Celie to Avey to us as readers provide guidance into our futures as black women brought in chains to a white-dominated and appropriated land.

To explain my critical framework in more detail, I take up in the following sections the issues I see as central to an empowered reading of diasporic literature by women. One of the first principles that I encountered in my examination of these four texts, an idea that fundamentally shaped my understanding of them, is that the history of slavery permeates their individualized narratives. It is this reality with which these writers must deal in order to examine truthfully the lives of their female characters. Without being aware of that history, we as readers will not grasp what these writers are about nor will we understand their characters. Furthermore, it is crucial that we recognize that this history of subjugation has been written by those who positioned themselves as record keepers, namely those who benefited from slavery. As Claude Levi-Strauss says: "historical facts are no more given than any other. It is the historian, or the agent of history, who constitutes them."[4] People of the African diaspora, while being victimized by these systems, were denied the inclusion of their perspective in the chronicling of their suppression. Black women writers, therefore, must first reclaim the perspective of their people and give a voice to the long-silenced experiences of the past, which is especially true for contemporary writers who now have the benefit of Afrocentric historical scholarship.

Nowhere is this reclamation more necessary than in the slave narrative, which is not just a record of subjugation and restraint but a source of redefinition in the way we view slavery's impact. Although the slave narratives were a conscious effort to end the evils of slavery, it is important to recognize that they were specific constructs of which persons, behaviors, and degrees of individual expression were thought of as deserving to be heard. This selection process inherently distorts our view of slaves, but although experiences of one slave often were used problematically as representative of the entire group, it is possible to liberate to some degree the repressed voices of others for whom the slave spoke. In addition, the complexities of the individual voice, although weighed down by stereotypes that devalued the capabilities of blacks in general, remained firmly intact.

Toni Morrison makes rememory or reconstruction of a distorted historical moment central to her novel *Beloved*, which is based on an account of a slave, Margaret Garner, who killed her child in 1856. Historical events as presented in the newspaper article Morrison recovered are not unlike the version of history as presented in Mary Prince's narrative, for both recount atrocities of slavery while suppressing the voice of the individual. However, unlike Mary Prince's story, which managed to convey her perspective on slavery, the voice of Margaret Garner is almost entirely missing as the white reporter relays only those aspects of Garner's life that are consistent with his white audience's preconceptions. While it is noted that her preacher mother-in-law, for instance, understood the pain that led Garner to infanticide as an escape for her children, the only time Garner herself is quoted is to address the question of her sanity.

These selected parts of the reporter's conversation with Garner say nothing of who her master was and what her actual suffering entailed, nor do they shed light on how she and other slaves so brutalized by slavery got through such an existence. Most importantly the article does not address the contradictions inherent in the value of life for a slave, which was on one hand conceptualized by Christian masters as a precious gift from God, while on the other it was devalued by slavery and brutal acts of the very people who professed to believe in that same God. Garner's complex act of infanticide is only known through the white prism of the reporter P.S. Bassett who piously tells us: "As I listen to the facts, and witness the agony depicted in her countenance, I could not but exclaim,

Oh, how terrible is irresponsible power, when exercised over intelligent beings!"[5]

The meaning of surviving and confronting an existence of subjugation from the perspective of Margaret Garner, a female slave, is not found in this document of history, Morrison demonstrates, but in the historical memories preserved in legacies, traditions, and rituals kept alive in the black community. In *Beloved*, historical memory gives voice to Margaret Garner's silenced perspective and redefines it as one of female revolt. It provides some sense of Garner's story, moreover, as connected to/expressive of the suffering of sixty million or more, nameless but remembered. All the characters of the novel, through their memories of slavery, come to embrace the history of suffering they had blotted out of their conscious minds and thereby heal themselves enough from its legacy to love each other as well as themselves.

In *Beloved*, Toni Morrison gives Margaret Garner a voice, a past, a mind, and a heart in the character of Sethe. Sethe is a woman of great courage and humanity who took control of her situation, counter to all the constructed and legal strategies that bound her. Although her sanity is challenged, as we saw with her historical antecedent, it is Sethe's humanity which rejects an insane world that has no respect for human beings. She desperately yet bravely articulates to the ghost of her baby why she took her life as a means of saving it, and, through this fictionalized conversation, Toni Morrison provides Margaret Garner with the voice denied her in the historical record. Haunted by a life of separation from her mother, the bestiality of her owners' nephews, and the brutality of slavery, Sethe defeats her fears to secure the right of her child not to endure an existence which was, in effect, unlivable. The consequences of her act of revolt required no greater suffering than would have been the pain of bringing a child into a world that would eventually kill her body and her spirit. Sethe's strength, courage, and conviction, as presented in her time spent with the earthly presence of her dead baby, clearly shows she rejects forgiveness from others, for it is the right to speak and be understood that she seeks to claim.

Sethe's story, although the main focus of Morrison's attempt to validate Margaret Garner, is echoed to varying degrees by other female characters in the novel. These women, while reflecting on the part of their circumstances that are similar to Sethe's, recall either aborting or rejecting their children after birth because their inability to protect their children from a life of slavery was a painful reality. The struggle to have a say in the lives of their children is presented at length with our understanding of the determination that leads Baby Suggs to track down her lost children and her pain when she encounters the insanity that claims the only child she could locate, Sethe's husband. It is indeed the women of the community's recognition of these painful experiences as acts of revolt in a powerless situation that causes them to come to Sethe's aid.

Sethe, in confronting her own painful memories, seeks what other characters in the novel do not recognize they can claim— understanding—because she has already forgiven herself for an act produced by a choiceless situation. As the characters forgive and understand Sethe, they soon learn to embrace and forgive themselves for their own powerlessness in the face of slavery and its problem-filled aftermath. As the community comes to terms with Sethe's essential goodness and embraces her as a member, it slowly removes the barriers to painful recall of its enslaved history. Only in opening themselves to collective memory can these ex-slaves begin the healing process that will allow them to love each other unreservedly. Morrison thus connects Margaret Garner's individual suffering to that of black people as a whole, divided by their refusal to remember a past too painful to contemplate. As Toni Morrison so movingly demonstrates in *Beloved*, when female characters allow the past to surface from their unconscious minds, they can process the memory of slavery into a strengthening guide for the future. As Gloria Hull states:

> African Diasporan people—[have been]—brought in chains to foreign islands and chilly shores — kidnapped, raped, oppressed, colonized. We have survived all that not only to document the original, terrible journey, but to take the literal and metaphoric trip back home.[6]

Morrison creates this journey home for us and in the process demonstrates another important theme for women writers of the diaspora: the importance of folktales, songs, rituals, stories, and family lore for reclaiming a silenced history. To recognize this cultural treasure trove, however, black people must overcome yet another obstacle created by a white double standard. Although written history has been the major source of information about the past for whites, the preservation of historical events through a collective, oral memory has been considered a valid process for many dominant culture thinkers; yet these same analysts have ignored its validity for people who have been oppressed by racism. G.W.F. Hegel posed memory as the antecedent/threshold to civilization but also limited its usefulness when discussing the African.[7] Henry Louis Gates Jr. disputes Hegel's position, stating that:

> Hegel's strictures on the African about the absence of "history" presume a crucial role of memory — of a collective, cultural memory — in the estimation of a civilization. [But] metaphor of the childlike nature of the slaves, of the masked, puppetlike personality of the black, all share [an] assumption about the absence of memory.[8]

French historian Pierre Nora amplifies Gates's critique of Hegel when he states: "the quest for memory is the search for history."[9] Nora's concept is further explored by Melvin Dixon, who discusses memory as an appropriate tool for the recovery of a cultural context for black people. In his essay "The Black Writer's Use of Memory," he states:

> the presence in our culture of significant *lieux de mémoire* [events that cause one to remember: sites of memory] establishes the value of cultural memory and the kind of history or historiography that is not dependent on written analysis or criticism but rather achieves an alternative record of critical discussion through the exercise of memory. Memory becomes a tool to regain and reconstruct not just the past but history itself.[10]

This perspective illuminates Morrison's use of memory as a viable tool for constructing a "larger picture" of history for the diaspora and its writers. Her validation of folklore, myth, ghosts, and other representations of the black past opens paths for her characters who have been erased from written history and brings black people into the universe of civilizations with a rich oral history.

Like Morrison, Alice Walker reconstitutes an actual historic event in portraying the murder of a black storekeeper by a white mob in *The Color Purple* with an eye toward an empowered ending to the story.[11] In this case, the daughter of the murdered man ends up owning the store herself. Celie overcomes the silence of her historical counterpart and the fear of her community to construct a living memory of black female resistance to the erasure of her history. In reclaiming a history in which black voices are at the center of events, diasporic writers such as Walker and Morrison, along with narrators such as Mary Prince, testify to the importance of this kind of individual empowerment, yet they also contend with another common element: the interaction of a segregated community with recovery of individual memory and power. We see in Mary Prince's narrative that the community is backgrounded, for instance, but by broadening our sense of Mary's individual history it becomes clear that the community is instrumental in defining Mary's sense of her own value. In *Beloved*, similarly, the community is necessary to Sethe's healing journey from isolated sufferer to whole human being. In both of these texts, community support emerges as a crucial factor in the ultimate success of their female protagonists in contesting the white power structure's version of history.

Walker takes a somewhat more complex stance on the role of community in black women's lives by describing ambiguities and silences within black society. Because black people have been subjected to punishment as a consequence of those who challenge white rule, their communities have often responded in ambiguous ways to those who appear radically individualistic. This caution toward radical acts of defiance produced by lynchings, beatings, and unjust imprisonment serves as the catalyst in *The Color Purple* for Celie's initial victimization. The murder of Celie's father, whose success was a threat to whites, caused Celie to lose the protection of her family and made her vulnerable.[12] Celie is not encouraged by the community to develop a positive identity in part because it has witnessed the brutal suppression of individual power by jealous whites. Its erasure of her personal history mirrors its own amnesia, adopted out of self-protection and fear. It is, significantly, a radically individualistic black woman, Shug, who helps Celie regain her true heritage and shows her how to overcome community repression and silence. Once Celie is able to express herself, in turn, she moves the community forward in its acknowledgment of both her family's and Mr.--'s illegitimate abuse of her. Walker shows, then, that the loss of historical memory or denial of it segments the black community and potentially paralyzes it through perpetuating destructive and damaging behaviors within the community itself.

Paule Marshall's *Praisesong for the Widow* reconstructs an important historical moment as well, one she redefines as inspirational for modern-day black women. Marshall presents a legend passed on to Avey Johnson by her Great-aunt Cuney about a group of Ibos brought to Tatem, Georgia, as slaves who boldly picked up their chains and walked on the water back home to Africa. In this case, Marshall explores the importance of legends through the character of Great-aunt Cuney who adopts the Eurocentric version of history that invalidates such stories but who gradually recenters herself as an African-based woman with a rich history of traditions and rituals. Marshall not only shows Avey, the main character, reclaiming the rituals and historical memories of her ancestral past but she presents Great-aunt Cuney as a self-affirming woman who evaluates traditions and rituals positively. What Great-aunt Cuney demands of Avey is she remember that traditions and rituals are protection against cultural erasure, a condition Avey indeed falls into in her quest for middle-class success. The one paramount lesson that Great-aunt Cuney teaches Avey involves, in fact, an Africanized Christian ritual called the ringshout. She recognizes it as one step in the progression toward freedom and cultural reclamation that is be learned from without betraying oneself. It is Great-aunt Cuney's refusal not to dance in the ringshout of her church, a stance secured by her understanding of how African rituals adapted to Christianization, that helps Avey move backward to reclaim a lost heritage from the Caribbean Islanders she meets on a vacation. For the characters in *Praisesong*, modern America need not be a place where African tradition is forgotten in order to escape poverty. Avey Johnson finds that the history of her people is a far more important treasure than any material wealth and that until she can locate herself within that history, she is a hollow, invisible woman without goals or roots.

As we have seen from our examination of these four women writers from the diaspora, the impact of historical erasure and the legacy of slavery cannot be ignored if we are to understand clearly what their texts are doing. Similarly, an awareness of this history is crucial for illuminating the significance of language in their writings. Because of the drastic curtailment of freedom, language became the only available source of protection against their oppressors for newly enslaved Africans. Since the use of African languages was prohibited, the unfamiliar tongue of whites had to be adopted to deal with the even more unfamiliar circumstance of subjugation. As Geneva Smitherman states:

> The condition of servitude and oppression contributed to the necessity for coding or disguising English from the white man. Since slaves were forced to communicate in the white man's tongue, they had to devise ways of runnin it down that would be powerful and meaningful to the black listener, but harmless and meaningless to any whites who might overhear their rap.[13]

The dual purpose of communication necessitated a manipulation of words, images, and meanings that would protect slaves from some listeners while revealing their true intentions to others in a dangerous balancing act. The speaker reached out to two audiences and conveyed multiple meanings in a complex system by using a singular arrangement of words. Masking, which is what this manipulation of language is called, is a crucial component in the linguistic history of the African American as Henry Louis Gates Jr. states in *Figures in Black*:

> Of course, with slavery and the evolution of the slave songs into spirituals, the mask was utilized in a political context--indeed, as a matter of personal safety--to say one thing, all the while meaning another, usually under the guise of religious expression.[14]

English for the slave was thus adapted to focus on survival concerns first, and public communication of personal perspectives was secondary since the ownership of self seemed such a remote possibility while the audience itself was untrustworthy.

As blacks became more aware of the philosophies and the system of oppression that encompassed their lives as slaves, language, too, was recognized as a tool for abolishing that system. For slaves, the language that gave a true sense of how they felt about their circumstance was appropriate and safe for their community but not for the audience of whites who could end the heinous system of slavery. In slave narratives such as that of *The History of Mary Prince, A West Indian Slave*, therefore, language is politically constructed and carefully slanted toward the sympathies of an enlightened but still unreliable audience. Because the goal was the social and political education of only white readers, it is not entirely accurate to say such texts are an example of masking. However, because the slave narrative was under the watchful eye of white sponsors, the speaker had to suppress the "natural" language used among blacks in favor of a formal, distanced discourse that would serve the same protective function of masking. Mary Prince's account of subjugation is exemplary of a narrative voice that cannot be too frank regarding individual perspectives of the author but must remain carefully focused on abolitionist goals. She had to explore the political essence of personal events while maintaining a subordinated distance from her white listeners. Her narrative, like others, sought to inform and provoke outrage and not to reveal deeply internal aspects of her life as a black woman.

While Emancipation brought legal freedom of expression to blacks, the continuation of racist exclusion and oppression meant that masking continued as a defense against the white majority. Simultaneously, black dialect, which developed out of the remnants of slave language, began to reflect a world view set apart from that contained in the language from which it arose. For the writer of the diaspora and particularly for the African American writer, the assumption that literature must conform to white language standards had to be revised in order to incorporate the black vernacular so expressive of a distinctly black perspective on life. Consider the debate that African American scholars of the Harlem Renaissance waged over whether art should be for art's sake or should present an idealized picture of African American people.[15] The use of dialect was central to this debate, for some writers like Zora Neale Hurston insisted on presenting black life as it was, not as white America envisioned morality, success, or good character. Others like Jessie Fauset were uncomfortable with Hurston's vernacular as they believed exposure of community language to a white audience would reinforce racist stereotypes.[16] Writers and scholars such as Alain Locke wanted dialect to remain in the African American community to avoid, among other things, "conscious posing and self-conscious sentimentality."[17] To expose this language exposure to both white and black readers weakened its protective aspect for the community, according to many black intellectuals, even though it liberated that same community from destructive silences.

These two issues--balancing personal expression with political goals and validating the black vernacular without reinforcing white stereotypes--permeate fictional texts of the twentieth century, and the three novels in this study explore them in particularly illuminating ways. It is important to recognize, first of all, that the fictional characters created by Morrison, Walker, and Marshall can convey a greater sense of linguistic complexity than can the slave narrative. What emerges from these novels, therefore, is a discourse that moves between past and present, public and private, in its rendering of the complex circumstance of slavery's legacy. Plurality and often ambiguity are particularly prevalent in women's writing because women's reproductive role and gender oppression have complicated their struggles with racism. Their double jeopardy, so to speak, has made for them even more important the following concept articulated by Pat Hill Collins: "Knowledge without wisdom is adequate for the powerful, but wisdom is essential to the survival of the subordinate."[18] The wisdom of these three texts is that they openly express long-silenced voices and expose concealed knowledge without committing themselves to one interpretation of the black experience or revealing, in a reckless way, the painful reality of their characters.

In *Beloved*, for instance, the narrative voice allows the reader into the characters' world, but the focus primarily is on the impact of the experience on the character not the edification of a white reader. In addition, the reader is assumed to be somewhat familiar with or at least open to a black context, but elaborative details are revealed only as he or she commits to the text. An example of my point is that at one juncture, a memory of Beloved's experience on a slave ship is presented as she perceives it while still a very young child, alone and afraid. The language does not encourage a swift and uncomplicated resolution of her horrific situation but instead focuses on Beloved's child-like, powerless perspective. This technique forces the reader to identify with a slave child in the hold of a ship well into the narrative, without relief from her pain or confusion. The recreation of this historic memory of the Middle Passage from the perspective of the innocent and the enslaved simultaneously gives voice to a silenced historical episode while conveying the notion that absence of language adequate to describe the experience was a key element of the horror. The reader's nearly alienated state as he or she struggles to understand the inchoate language of the text parallels the alienation of the character herself from a world that has erased her voice and brutalized her body. Moreover, the layers of meaning that lie within Morrison's text go far beyond the literal language and force the reader to provide an Afrocentric historical perspective in order to understand it.

Alice Walker uses a similar technique in *The Color Purple* when she thrusts the reader into the world view of an abused, voiceless, black woman from the early years of this century without contextualizing the letters by which we get to know her. We hear Celie's words and see the world through her eyes when it is described in dialect untranscribed into grammatically correct prose for the reader. It is a technique that demands acceptance on the reader's part of Celie's validity as a colloquial speaker. In addition, when we first meet Celie, we are forced to identify with the first-person narrative of a woman without a voice, a woman like so many others, who is lost even within the closure of the black community. Celie's language, which is initially reflective of her child-like sense of the world, takes on power, richness, and authority as she assumes control of her life. She moves from speaking to her "white man" God to other women in her community who hear and value her voice. She moves from words and images that the world says represent her to a language that reflects self-love. One aspect of this transformation is that Celie must resist attempts to reform her speech patterns, remove her individualistic expressions, and adopt the standard English that is part of the very images that have erased her. As she replies to a friend who advises her to learn "proper" English: "Look like to me only a fool would want you to talk in a way that feel peculiar to your mind" (223). Celie's fractured grammar expresses her essence as survivor of a cruel world, itself fractured by racism, sexism, and imperialism. She has created it to name her own identity, and it is evidence of her hard-won power over the way her mind works, so it, like herself, must be left rough, honest, and full of wit.

Avey Johnson from *Praisesong for the Widow* in adopting a middle-class image to achieve the American dream is like the woman in *The Color Purple* who considers "proper" English essential for constructing an external presence that has little to do with internal truths. At first glance, it may seem as if Avey Johnson's appropriation of an identity and language acceptable to whites parallels Mary Prince's presentation of a depersonalized Christian persona in her abolitionist tract, but Marshall's literary purposes are quite different than those of the slave narrator. Marshall clearly shows, for one thing, that Avey needs to express her inner feelings whereas Mary has a rational rhetorical strategy that protects her internal reality from the intruding, biased eyes of readers with far more power than she. It is also the case that Mary did not relinquish her cultural roots to achieve her persona; rather she suppressed them temporarily for the safety of her people and the grander mission of freedom. For Avey and Jerome Johnson, a middle-class public persona *was* their grand mission, therefore their language had to nullify African cultural influences to meet the approval of a white majority. Unfortunately, only Avey Johnson survives to reclaim the legacy of her ancestral culture, while Jerome Johnson succumbs to the weight of suppressing and nullifying his own identity.

Although Avey has molded herself into the role of a middle-class black woman by adopting the Eurocentric language patterns of the dominant culture, we discover it is not the only discourse that has passed through her life. She remembers a black dialect (*patois*) and connects emotionally with the broken English of her Out-islander guide, Lebert Joseph. We see as Avey moves through the rituals and process of reclaiming her cultural identity that her language comes to reflect the unique aspects of her African ancestral past. Significantly, when Avey thinks of her empty past life and of the daughter whom she tried to abort, she asks for forgiveness in the way of the "Old Parents" by saying "Pádoné mwê" (255). Most importantly, she drops the culturally sterile name of Avey for the musical namesake of her grandmother, Avatara, given at birth. For Paule Marshall, then, language is inseparable from cultural pride and if moving up the American ladder to success means abandoning African cadences and metaphors, one will be left invisible and powerless to express the hidden self within.

The final dimension of my critical framework, one that is just as essential as the concepts of historical reclamation and the unusually complex issues involved in language choice, is that of image construction or, more accurately, revision. One stumbling block women authors of the diaspora must overcome is the bedrock of racist stereotypes that surround them as black women.[19] Not surprisingly a defining quality of their fiction is the struggle waged by their female characters to find a true reflection of who they are in a society that has thrown up so many distorted images.[20] Stereotypes such as that of Jezebel, the low-class seducer, have been used to justify the misuse and abuse of the black woman's body, and Aunt Jemima, the maternal though sexless maid, has been portrayed as totally devoted to white families and content in her role as servant, thereby justifying the exploitation of domestic workers. Since the Aunt Jemima image has been the most accommodating and has suggested unwavering obedience to white authority, this is the model most whites sought to perpetuate, so whatever positive qualities for black women that have been allowed to emerge are firmly rooted in the subservient maid role, a demeaning image of sexlessness and accommodation to inequality.

All stereotypes of black women in the dominant culture have distorted the personalities, skills, and cunning of those truly seeking equality and freedom. Aunt Jemima is the cook of undying loyalty who rolls her eyes in the stereotype, but in truth such women created stability for their own families through competent service to an employer. They knew the importance of their role economically and often served as intermediary between family or community and the white power structure. Sapphire, similarly, is portrayed as a loud and blistering individual in the stereotype, but in truth through persistence and assertiveness, black women encouraged others to take necessary action. Superwoman in the stereotype is deemed an emasculator since she is able to provide for her family when her man cannot, but in truth women have been the stabilizing force of the family and community when men are institutionally or economically separated from them.[21] The manipulation of these human and necessary attributes has loomed large over the real truth of black women's lives.

Many of the female characters within diasporic texts are trapped in limited and destructive existences rationalized by these stereotypes, which taint not only the perception of others but also the perspective they have of themselves as they internalize many of these images.[22] If we explore the specific ways this process works in the three novels under examination, we find that one crucial factor in loss of identity is the stripping away of family or ancestral heritage, which removes a crucial defense against these negative images. Without family or community resistance on the character's behalf, she cannot seek her own identity with so little in her world that recognizes her individual value or beauty. Celie in *The Color Purple*, for instance, though knowing she has a past that predates the tyranny of Mr.-- and Pa, is alienated from it by the systems of oppression manifested in the brutal murder of her father, the abuse of her body, and the rejection of her personal worth by virtue of her dark skin.[23] She has no real connection to a female past to debunk the ugly stereotypes that conceal her beauty or potential. Celie also sees many women in her world who have tried to move past these stereotypes and failed. Sofia, trapped in the "maid role," tried to reject it, but the effort cost her a severe beating and years of imprisonment and servitude. Anna Julia, in an even worse fate, has her life destroyed by the violence that often erupts when a black woman seeks to escape her limits.

Similarly, in *Beloved* the character of the young woman, Beloved, is victimized by the perception that black women are sexual objects to be used at will by white men. Having been trapped most of her life as the concubine of her master, Beloved rebels, but she kills her captor only to be loose in a world that has already killed the one source of identification and safety she had, her mother. Without the guidance of her female ancestral past, Beloved does not know her own face when she looks at her reflection in a stream. Symbolizing how important her lost mother is to her process of self-reclamation, Beloved thinks the reflection is her mother's face, but she will not be able to recognize her own features before finding a mother substitute in the form of Sethe and thereby reconnecting with a past that can nurture her identity.

Avey Johnson in *Praisesong for the Widow*, unlike Beloved and Celie, has in her historical memory traditions, rituals, stories, and songs for her guidance, but they are instead repressed. Avey also has Great-aunt Cuney, who, as the female ancestral presence in her life, insists that she not fall victim to the confusion and alienation that the world seeks to place before black women. However, although Avey learns all about her ancestral past early in life, she is swayed by the stereotypes and images of what she must *not* be in order to be successful. She has internalized the stereotypes that go with being black, being poor, and being without a man, in large part because she and her husband embrace the American dream of success, abandoning the truths of the African American community of Harlem for a white suburb. It is no wonder that upon seeing her own reflection in a mirror while having dinner on a cruise that she, like Beloved, does not recognize herself. Her perspective of self has been so whitewashed in trying to achieve the white majority's criteria of success that her own reflection startles her by how much she has changed. Avey must retrieve lessons learned from the Ibos, who took control of their own destiny and thus their own image, as to base her identity on what others define as happiness dooms her to a life so repressed that death, as Avey's husband comes to know, is the only relief.

In these novels, stereotypes must first be confronted and then deconstructed, rejected, and replaced with strong portraits of real women who have evolved beyond the limits of others' distortions.[24] Sofia, for example, in *The Color Purple* defies the image of herself in white society as a maternal figure devoted to her white charges. Instead she overtly rejects mothering Janie's child and clearly prefers taking care of her own family, something she is restricted from doing by the white woman who selfishly limits her visits home. Alice Walker is revising here a stereotype to show the woman underneath just as she reveals the vulnerable, loving woman who is Shug, outwardly a Jezebel. Similarly, the maternal figure in *Beloved*, Baby Suggs, uses her energy to heal the black people of her community, not to take care of the personal troubles of whites. Finally, Great-aunt Cuney in *Praisesong for the Widow* breaks out of the stereotype of a humble, devoted Christian believer by questioning her church's prohibition against dance in the ringshout and many dominant culture assertions about her race's docility.

While revising these stereotypes, the three writers develop a major theme of women rejecting the damaging images constructed of them by tuning into survival knowledge passed on by female relations and friends. Women helping women is portrayed as a lifeline that reclaims those women isolated and abused. Sethe is a transitional character in *Beloved* who moves from slavery to emancipation and survives because Baby Suggs provides the foundation that sustains her, teaching her the beauty of being a creation of God who can only be fully realized by shaking off man's ugly illusions. Celie in *The Color Purple* must meet a similar challenge in freeing herself from bondage by realizing that her worth is not a function of the degree to which she resembles the stereotypical constructs of black women. This is a liberation that occurs through the help of Shug Avery, who has defied such stereotypes herself and shows Celie what it means to be loved by a woman. Shug, Nettie, Sofia, and other women in the community give Celie a way out of the patriarchal household that isolates her. Finally as Avey Johnson reclaims her past and allows her cultural identity to emerge, we see that she is supported by female ancestors such as Great-aunt Cuney as well as Lebert Joseph, the Out-lander who invites Avey on a metaphorical trip back to her cultural roots. Also instrumental in her recovery of self are the women on the boat who help her survive the purgative sea-sickness that overwhelms her and the women who ritually rub and oil her body as one does a child growing into her physical self and sense of the world. All these characters are able to move past the stereotypes and illusions of a black woman to a greater sense of themselves, largely through the aid of other women.

Mary Prince's exception to the thematic treatment of stereotype deconstruction and self-development in the contemporary novels analyzed here is rooted, I believe, in her having been armed with the knowledge of her own worth and the boundless potential of black women through African legacies that were a part of her life. She flatly recognized that the violent and degrading behavior of others was not acceptable on any level, whether the victim was herself or not. Mary Prince knew of her ancestral past and her immediate history to a degree not possible for the fictional women farther removed in time from Africa and more thoroughly distanced from it by the nature of their societies. Furthermore, she knew she was not free and had no illusions of free choice, so she could be more completely on guard against assaults. Her fictional sisters, on the other hand, have been told they are free, yet they encounter stereotypes that can hold them down in invisible ways. They are, therefore, in some ways more dependent on other women for support in constructing empowering reflections to combat the false ones.

To summarize, what we need to keep in mind when reading these and other texts by women of the diaspora is that written history has excluded the perspective of African American people while devaluing their historical memories. Ancestral memory, on the other hand, has served as both protection from and guidance through the outside world and preserver of experiences within the community for people with African roots. This dual nature of history from the perspective of the African American informs us that, in Geneviève Fabre and Robert O'Meally's words:

> The legacy of slavery and the serried workings of racism and prejudice have meant that even the most optimistic black Americans are, as the expression goes, "born knowing" that there is a wide gulf between America's promises and practices. For blacks this tragic consciousness has spelled a cautious and critical attitude toward unfolding experience--a stance toward history that is braced by the awareness that the past, as Faulkner put it, has never really *passed.*[25]

It thus becomes necessary that we recognize the interaction between official historical records and politically subjugated people as a process that largely excludes African American voices but has the potential to present the past in an enlightening way.

In looking at the historical aspects of the texts discussed in this work and how they use cultural legacies and oral accounts to expand the perspectives of the characters, it is necessary to validate memory as a resource for chronicling the past. All of the novels discussed here rely on memory not only to recall the immediate past but to retrieve ancestral voices as well, and they encourage us to expand our perspective of history to include those who have been distorted by or erased from the written record. Toni Morrison especially calls for removal of the veil over certain facts of African American history in her work.[26] She employs imagination as it is bound up in the memory of her characters to reveal and liberate history's silences.

When we consider that written history has been narrowly focused on a select group of voices to the detriment of people of color and their diverse forms of communication, we must keep in mind that those previously excluded express ideas in ways that are necessarily imbued with a multiplicity of meanings. As Geneviève Fabre and Robert O'Meally state in their analysis of African American expression, there is caution in the way someone vulnerable to racism unfolds experience with language.[27] This awareness of vulnerability has produced language in black texts that is multileveled and even ambiguous at times. When we examine diasporic texts that preference women as protagonists and, in turn, allow the female voice to be a narrative guide, we see a second layer of protective language that codes female rebellion into seemingly acquiescent women, both real and fictional. We must read texts by women of the diaspora, then, with an eye toward the multidimensionality they express in language choice while being sensitive to the risks they are taking in making community knowledge available to an outside audience.

It is also important to recognize that the black woman protagonist has had to reclaim her own truths from the attitudes and expectations of those around her. We recognize even in the slave narrative that proclaims individual authorship through titles such as "Related by Herself" that the author must contend with a societal structure of dominance based on race, class and gender, one that, in Hazel Carby's view, profoundly determines the degree to which her voice can be heard.[28] The female protagonist thus steps into an arena where she must confront a past structured on the privileges of affluent white men in order to redefine her present, but her voice, we discover, is capable of speaking about, defining, and recreating the experiences that are distorted or erased by white patriarchal constructs.[29]

These are some of the major issues I see impacting our appreciation of black women writers as they struggle to fashion a positive female identity. In sorting through these issues, I have found the following critics to be the most helpful in articulating what that identity is. Barbara Christian is one of many African American scholars who explore viable critical theories that place the black female voice in an identifiable literary tradition, but she does so with an eye toward viable models for contemporary readers.[30] Gayatri Spivak in her critical look at female texts discusses the verbal and social significance of texts that she sees as not merely a reflection of sociological reality but a call as well for social change.[31] bell hooks provides a female voice that is fully liberated as she speaks emphatically on her own behalf and directly to her listener.[32] With language as only one means of expressing circumstance and identity, Hortense Spillers adds to our picture by calling upon the reader to recognize the shifting and sometimes contradictory aspects of a black female voice that is sometimes at odds with language itself.[33] Finally Kari J. Winter seems to conflate the goals of woman author and slave narrator as she concludes from her study of women's literature that all such women seem to write/right their own stories.[34] All of these critics attest to the complexity of black women's writing over time and to their empowering messages.

The diasporic literature I have examined suggests that the past of subjugated peoples need no longer be a silencing reign of terror but is a resource that can be plumbed for empowering images of African people brought to the Americas. At the same time, it shows that although time has done away with the political reality of slavery, its internal baggage, often denied, continues to be carried destructively into contemporary times. The texts I have discussed look to the cultural past of dispersed Africans' lives and seek to dismantle, explore, and, most importantly, not deny these horrific experiences. As painful as this past is, it must be understood as a chronicle of survival of a group threatened by genocide and psychological crippling which, against the greatest of odds, has maintained its cultural heritage. These texts strive to excavate truths that may not always be specific as to names and dates but are historically enlightening because they are embraced by the black community in its collective memory. From exploring diasporic experiences written, remembered, whispered, and feared, these women writers show us that the human condition does not always produce nobility and love, but that it is possible out of sacrifice, determination, and self-acceptance to achieve those things. They demonstrate that African American literature by women is about writing oneself free. From the slave narrative to the most postmodern of contemporary novels, women writers have created an avenue of change and a resource for healing that lies at our fingertips to set the process of reclamation and wholeness into motion.

Although all of the female voices in these four texts, to return to the narratives themselves, are courageous examples of overcoming emotional hurdles constructed by slavery and the ensuing loss of Afrocentric perspectives, I find the most inspirational character to average black women in their effort to find a place in the world is Celie in *The Color Purple*, whose struggle reaches the quiet recesses of those oppressed women whose voices, so long silenced, have so very much to say. Celie is, as well, a combination of all the other characters, for she is initially ignorant of her history as is Beloved; she finds guidance from other women as does Sethe; she reclaims her past as does Avey Johnson; and she takes control of her life as does Mary Prince. Celie also demonstrates how important community support is to the development of black women, for, while she is trapped by its patriarchal values and destructive silences, she cannot move beyond others' definition of who she is. Celie's experience, above all, shows that recovery of one's family ancestry is possible, retrieval of African heritage can be achieved, and the self can be empowered to reject abuse even under the most daunting of circumstances. In this way, she embodies all the major themes addressed by these four writers and all the strengths that help us as readers define the future.

In conclusion, as the black woman begins to come to terms with her own identity and the images she would choose to embrace, she questions through historical retrieval, multilayered language, and raising her own voice the roles imposed on herself and her sisters. As is so well stated by Toni Morrison:

> she had nothing to fall back on: not maleness, not whiteness, not ladyhood, not anything. And out of the profound desolation of her reality she may well have invented herself.[35]

In her self-invention, the black woman continues to free herself from the one-dimensionality of stereotyped images toward an individuality which speaks to, about, and for her people but also for herself. She continues to create an image and an identity carved from the souls and sacrifices of her sisters--known, unknown, dreamed of, and hoped for.

As we see in the various texts discussed here, an Afrocentric historicized identity is the essence of black women, who, when whole and healthy, are empowered to no longer submit to others' images but instead commit to their own agenda. This is the process of evolution toward wholeness that characters from a wide variety of women authors strive to achieve. We learn from them that it is the hard choices of life that strengthen one, and it is possible to reclaim a place in one's family, culture, or community even if one has strayed from diasporic wisdom or been broken by the weight of subjugation. The black woman, bruised, abandoned, betrayed, and used, ultimately chooses to put forth her own image of who she is in these texts--struggling and kicking against the imposition of others. Maya Angelou says it best:

> You may write me down in history
> With your bitter, twisted lies,
> You may trod me in the very dirt
> But still, like dust, I'll rise ... [36]

And so the women of the diaspora write, expanding history, seeking those voices which make clear their image, and embracing those identities that allow them to exist on their own terms.

Notes

1. Quoted in Geneviève Fabre and Robert O'Meally, *History and Memory in African-American Culture* (New York: Oxford University Press, 1994), 64.

2. Slavery in early women's texts is seen in novels such as Frances E.W. Harper, *Iola Leroy* (1892); Pauline Hopkins, *Contending Forces* (1900); and again in Jessie Fauset's novels *Plum Bun* (1929) and *The Chinaberry Tree* (1931). Harper used slavery to discuss the injustices and degradation that freed black Americans suffered at the hands of the white majority, while providing a narrative forum to promote social change. Hopkins used history to raise questions about cultural inheritance, while Fauset tried to present a new relationship to history for her middle-class characters. A strong sense of history is also evident in the political writings of Anna Julia Cooper, *A Voice from the South* (1892), and Ida B. Wells in her pamphlet "A Red Record: Tabulated Statistics and Alleged Causes of Lynching in the United States, 1892-1894" (1895), along with many other pamphlets and short essays in her fight against lynching.

3. The exception to this is Zora Neale Hurston, who addressed the rural black female's search for individuality using vernacular language directly influenced by cultural cadences. Hurston used language to bring perspectives of the text closer to that of the people about whom she wrote and to give a more accurate sense of the black female voice, but she did not do so with the political depth achieved by modern writers. Since the Harlem Renaissance was as much a political as a literary upheaval aimed at black people's visibility, the presentation of blacks as idealized as well-assimilated citizens was an issue placed before the black artist at every turn. Hurston, known as a woman who spoke her mind, chose freedom of expression but was highly criticized for her literary choice.

4. Claude Levi-Strauss, *The Savage Mind* (Chicago: University of Chicago Press, 1966), 257.

5. Middleton Harris, Morris Levitt, Roger Furman, and Ernest Smith, eds. *The Black Book* (New York: Random House, 1974), 10.

6. Gloria T. Hull, "The Black Woman Writer and the Diaspora," *The Black Scholar*, vol. 17 no. 2 (March/April 1986), 2-4.

7. G.W.F. Hegel, *The Philosophy of History* (New York: Dover Publications, 1956), 91-99. Hegel states regarding the African: "What we properly understand by African, is the Unhistorical, Undeveloped Spirit, still involved in the conditions of mere nature, and which had to be presented here only as on the threshold of the world's History."

8. Henry Louis Gates, Jr., *Figures in Black: Words, Signs, and the "Racial" Self* (New York: Oxford University Press, 1987), 20.

9. Pierra Nora quoted by Melvin Dixon, "Between Memory and History: *Les Lieux de Memoire*," *Representations* 26 (Spring 1989), 7-24.

10. Melvin Dixon, "The Black Writer's Use of Memory," Fabre and O'Meally, *History and Memory*, 18-19.

11. Alice Walker has taken her incident from an historical account described by Paula Giddings, who begins her history of black women in America with the story of Thomas Moss, a black storekeeper in Memphis, Tennessee, who was lynched in 1892. The incident is further described in Chapter 4 of this study. *When and Where I Enter: The Impact of Black Women on Race and Sex in America* (New York: Bantam Books, 1984), 17-18.

12. The life of isolation that Celie experiences is reflective of a folk saying shared with Walker by her sister. As stated in Walker's book, *In Search of Our Mother's Gardens*, she found the idea for *The Color Purple* in an anecdote told to her by her sister Ruth: "One day the Wife asked The Other Woman for a pair of her drawers." Although Walker doesn't elaborate on the anecdote, we do know that it involves the relationship of one man and two women. The silence that is broken with this statement removes a barrier that isolated the women from one another and moves them toward the sharing of knowledge and the potential for personal growth made possible by women helping women. We see this connection between Celie and Shug as each woman helps the other to remove herself from the control of Mr. -- to a life that is self-defined. (New York: Harcourt Brace Jovanovich, 1983), 355.

13. Geneva Smitherman, *Talkin and Testifyin: The Language of Black America* (Detroit: Wayne State University Press, 1977), 47.

14. Gates, *Figures*, 175.

15. This debate between black critics, the intelligentsia, and the writers themselves is described in Cary D. Wintz, *Black Culture and the Harlem Renaissance* (Houston: Rice University Press, 1988), 133 and 152.

16. Fauset never imposed her views on others but focused her work on middle-class characters to avoid reinforcing such stereotypes. She is discussed by Wintz, *Black Culture*, 152. The use of dialect was challenged by many critics and scholars as discussed by Esther Nettles Rauch in her review of the life of Paul Laurence Dunbar, an African American poet who wrote in black dialect: "For an African American to perpetuate in his art a stereotype that blacks themselves were struggling against was viewed by African scholars as inexcusable. Although their image may not have been entirely false, it was but one of many dimensions of black society; other aspects of black America were not presented, or they were overshadowed by that one image. Valerie Smith, Lea Baechler, and A. Walton Litz, eds. in *African American Writers: Profiles of Their Lives*

and *Works from the 1700's to the Present* (New York: Collier Books, 1993), 70-71.

17. Alain Locke's comments refer to the poetry of Paul Laurence Dunbar. The debate over Dunbar's use of dialect is discussed by Rauch in her review of Dunbar's life. *African American Writers*, 71.

18. Patricia Hill Collins, *Black Feminist Thought* (New York: Routledge, 1991), 208.

19. Deborah Gray White, *Arn't I a Woman: Female Slaves in the Plantation South* (New York: Norton Press, 1985). White challenges the stereotypes that were relegated to female slaves as constructs supportive of slavery itself and the masculine notion of gender roles. These images are the basis of stereotypes that continue to plague black women today.

20. These stereotypes are described well by Michelle Wallace, *Invisibility Blues: From Pop to Theory* (New York: Verso, 1990), 137-145. Wallace discusses the historical invisibility of the slave woman's role and asks, "How is the author to give the story in which she [black woman slave] is the center of intelligence a broad enough perspective to support the omniscient tone so characteristic of the historical novel?" She is here referring to the work of Margaret Walker, but this study will try to provide a more complete answer to that question.

21. An excellent discussion of this stereotype is provided by Michele Wallace, *Black Macho and the Myth of the Superwoman* (New York: Verso, 1990). A study that describes positive images of black women is Donald Bogle, *Brown Sugar: Eighty Years of America's Black Female Superstars* (New York: Da Capo Press, 1990).

22. Calvin C. Hernton notes that: "The personality, or ego, of the black woman is a product of and a response to all of the historical forces of American society ... [and] racism, or white supremacy, has had the most powerful effect ..." *Sex and Racism in America* (New York: Anchor Books, 1988), 133.

23. A good discussion of black identity in which the authors look at skin color as it has been incorporated in complex ways into the social structure of how blacks see each other is provided by Kathy Russell, Midge Wilson, and Ronald Hall, eds., *The Color Complex: The Politics of Skin Color Among African Americans* (New York: Anchor Books, 1992), 62-80.

24. Sondra O'Neale suggests that this process is characteristic of autobiography as well as fiction. "Reconstruction of the Composite Self: New Images of Black Women in Maya Angelou's Continuing Autobiography," *Black Women Writers (1950-1980): A Critical Evaluation*, ed. Mari Evans (New York: Anchor Books, 1984), 25-36.

25. Fabre and O'Meally, *History and Memory*, 3.

26. Toni Morrison discusses her perspective at length in "Site of Memory," *Inventing the Truth: The Art and Craft of Memoir*, ed. William Zinsser (Boston: Houghton Mifflin Company, 1987), 101-124.

27. Fabre and O'Meally, *History and Memory*, 3-5. This book was extremely helpful in solidifying my concept of historical memory and extending my research into language.

28. Hazel Carby, *Reconstructing Womanhood: The Emergence of the Afro-American Woman Novelist* (New York: Oxford University Press, 1987), 3-19.

29. bell hooks specifically discusses the white patriarchal imagery that distorts or erases black women's identity in *Outlaw Culture: Resisting Representations* (New York: Routledge, 1994), 73-81.

30. Barbara Christian, *Black Feminist Criticism: Perspectives on Black Women Writers* (New York: Pergamon Press, 1985). Also see Christian's "But What Do We Think We're Doing Anyway: The State of Black Feminist Criticism(s) or My Version of a Little Bit of History," *Changing Our Own Words: Essays on Croticism, Theory, and Writing by Black Women*, ed. Cheryl A Wall (New Brunswick, NJ: Rutgers University Press, 1991), 58-84; "Trajectories of Self-Definition: Placing Contemporary Afro-American Women's Fiction," *Conjuring: Black Women, Fiction and Literary Tradition*, eds. Marjorie Pryse and Hortense J. Spillers (Bloomington: Indiana University Press, 1985), 233-248. Other critics who put black women writers in a literary tradition are Deborah E. McDowell, *The Changing Same: Black Women's Literature, Criticism, and Theory* (Bloomington: Indiana University Press, 1995); Mari Evans, ed., *Black Women Writers, 1950-1980: A Critical Evaluation* (New York: Anchor Press, 1984; Hazel Carby, *Reconstructing Womanhood*, 1987; Mary Helen Washington, *Invented Lives: Narratives of Black Women 1860-1960* (New York: Anchor Press, 1987); Susan Willis, *Specifying: Black Women Writing the American Experience* (Madison: University of Wisconsin Press, 1987).

31. Gayatri Spivak, *In Other Words: Essays in Cultural Politics* (New York: Routledge, 1988), 102; "Can the Subaltern Speak?," *Marxism and The Interpretation of Culture*, eds. C. Nelson and L. Grossberg (Basingstroke, England: Macmillan Education, 1988), 271-313.

32. bell hooks, *Talking Back: Thinking Feminist—Thinking Black* (Boston: South End Press, 1989), 9.

33. Hortense Spillers, "Cross-Currents, Discontinuities: Black Women's Fiction," Pryse and Spillers, *Conjuring* 249-261.

34. Kari J. Winter, *Subjects of Slavery, Agents of Change: Women and Power in Gothic Novels and Slave Narratives 1790-1865* (Athens: University of Georgia Press, 1992), 30.

35. Toni Morrison, "What the Black Woman Thinks About Women's Lib," *New York Times Magazine*, Vol. 22 (August 1971), 63.

36. Maya Angelou, *And Still I Rise* (New York: Random House, 1978), 41.

CHAPTER 2

The History of Mary Prince,
A West Indian Slave, Related by Herself

History, Ancestry, and Identity

The slave narrative is a particularly important part of the tradition of African American literature as it has evolved from the necessity of survival experienced by oppressed persons while utilizing the language of slaves' capturers as a source of rebellion. The narrative serves as preface and foundation for continued expression of humanity and identity through fiction, poetry, and other literary genres. As the earliest written form of the captive Africans' experience, the slave narrative establishes identity as part of, as well as separate from, the unity. This is partly noted by the addition to the title of "Herself" or "Himself" that represents the individual as well as the collective experience of the enslaved.[1] We see these considerations carried forward into the contemporary works of not only America but the diaspora as a whole.[2] The slave narrative serves as a written protest of denied humanity for the dispossessed African as well as a conscious freeing of oneself through rational thought and the expression of experience through writing.[3] There are well-known slave narratives such as *The Interesting Narrative of the Life of Olaudah Equiano or Gustavus Vassa the African* (1789), *Narrative of the Life of Frederick Douglass* (1845), and *Incidents in the Life of a Slave Girl* (1861) by Harriet Jacobs. We may include among them *The History of Mary Prince, A West Indian Slave* (1831), which is not so well known but just as important in content and purpose.

Exploring experiences of both male and female slave narratives such as these brings clarity to all issues of oppression, as gender plays a key role in the kinds of restraints and forms of resistance recorded in these histories.[4] It is without question as well that gender cannot be separated from the writers' self-definitions. As noted, in particular, by Carole Boyce Davies regarding Afro-Caribbean/American women writers in "Writing

Home" [5]: "cultural politics have to be worked out along with sexual politics."[6] Mary Prince, in embracing her personal and community histories, provides an example of just such a gendered voice operating in both a public and a private sphere. Prince's narrative also is reflective of the working slave woman's experience, which broadens our understanding of the variety of individual responses to oppression, the wide range in acts of slave resistance, and the complex processes women slaves engaged in to achieve self-definition.[7]

Furthermore, the narrative of Mary Prince is a particularly ample resource for looking at the past as an historical reminder of the cultural, ancestral, and religious influences of Africa for people of the diaspora. Because of the geographic location of Mary Prince's childhood home on the island of Bermuda and its distinction in the Caribbean plantation system, Caribbean slaves had more opportunities for participating in their own maintenance than did North American slaves and had access to forming more self-contained societies.[8] These distinctions allow us to see some direct influences of African culture on the struggle of the slave for emancipation and self-actualization. It is worth reviewing in some detail, therefore, the conditions for slave resistance in Mary Prince's world.

Michael Mullin in his essay "Africans Name Themselves" discusses some distinctions found in the Caribbean system that differ from the Southern United States:

> Regional differences began immediately as new Negroes came ashore and, in the Caribbean, organized with shipmates and countrymen and later were placed as inmates on plantations. These moves set in motion an assimilation that remained African at its core. The pattern was sustained when new Negroes were given land for producing their own food, some of which was eventually sold in the dynamic internal markets dominated by slave women. No equivalent development occurred in the South, where shipmates, countrymen, and inmates were unheard of, and whites monopolized the marketing of food and most of its production.[9]

This distinction in circumstance allowed for a greater collective force of Africans, particularly African women, in the Caribbean who were somewhat self-reliant and able to continue ancestral and cultural traditions from their homeland. African traditions which supported community and self-preservation through resistance were a part of everyday life for all slaves but were more effectively present for people in the Caribbean. Resistance in both the American South and the Caribbean was often manifested through *maroons* or renegade fighters whose existence and success were a function of the country's terrain in which they found themselves.

> In each region maroonage depended on a terrain of
> relatively inaccessible wilderness, and the Southern
> frontier [U.S.] was vast and rugged. It was filled with
> formidable Indians and well-armed, land-hungry pioneers.
> In the Caribbean, geography was decisive. In Antigua --
> flat, treeless, and drying out -- maroonage never
> established itself .... But in the extensive mountains of
> Jamaica, maroons flourished.[10]

Both documented and oral histories have recorded the success of the
Maroons of Jamaica and the free island of Santo Domingo. Maroon
leaders such as Toussaint L'Ouverture and his allies were able to make
successful assaults on their oppressors because of access to secure hiding
places and the ability to be self-sufficient.[11] Islands such as Antigua and
Barbados were not geographically conducive to hiding and thus other
means for resistance were explored. Maroons in the Southern United
States were characterized as "vagabonds and bush fighters."[12] They were
not able to create a stable environment because they had to return to the
plantation for food and other necessary staples. This deterred more stable
communities from forming away from the brutality of the slaveholders.
For those who were able to create relatively self-reliant communities, the
tradition of family and culture played a focal part in maroon activity as it
did in all facets of the dispossessed African's life:

> as a means of easing the pain of displacement and the
> unintelligibility of capture, maroons struggled to
> reconstitute the traditional families to which all but the
> most assimilated of African Americans aspired. By
> including spirits of the dead as family, they managed to
> sustain old sanctions that in African fashion they put into
> "play"....[13]

These conscious efforts toward embracing traditional African culture
fostered respect for history and aided both personal and community
survival.

   One of the key factors in the shape resistance took was the numerical
ratio of white slaveholders to the slaves. In the Caribbean, blacks often
outnumbered whites while the demographics of the American South
varied.[14] In the American South, moreover, whites had easier access to
other communities and forces to put down any hint of insurrection or
resistance. This is also true of Caribbean locations that were
geographically unsuitable for hiding. Preserving community, culture and
traditions under these conditions was without a doubt a difficult but not
insurmountable task for slaves. For the enslaved African, this struggle has
marked his/her history with "contact and clash, amalgamation and
accommodation, resistance and change."[15]

   An example of this dynamic is the connection between British
slaveholders and the British empire which supported Mary Prince's

strategy of speaking out. Since slavery for the British empire existed in its colonized lands, its dependence on and exposure to slavery as part of their everyday life was not realized. This afforded a more distanced framework for perceiving slave resistance than held true in the American South. If anything, the British majority thought the colonial possessions were in need of humanitarian treatment as offered by the "civilized" to the "uncivilized." When behaviors by British subjects were inconsistent with this perception, the reputation of the subjects was blemished though not drastically so. Illustrating this tendency is William Wilberforce of the House of Lords who remarked that the only way to check colonial crimes was to "blazon them to the English public, and arm ourselves with public indignation."[16] Such a perspective constituted a classist rejection of those who participated in such "uncivilized" and "unchristian" behaviors that Mary spoke of in her narrative.

To contextualize further the significance of this text, Mary Prince was the first known black woman from British colonialist oppression who not only escaped slavery but had her experiences published in a text. *The History of Mary Prince, A West Indian Slave, Related by Herself* was published in 1831 by anti-slaver Thomas Pringle. The document confirmed the existence of atrocities toward blacks in the West Indies and added support to the movement for the abolition of slavery. In spite of its significance as a political and social document, Mary Prince's narrative has remained until recently a silenced and ignored part of history. Her first-hand account of the attitudes and oppressiveness of European plantocrats towards people of African descent exposes the inhumanity and immorality that stands in marked contrast to their assumed social and moral piety. It serves also as an open rejection of the claim that blacks were willing to remain enslaved. Many of the assumptions about blacks, then and now, rested on a conceived notion of inferiority. Colonists saw this as justification for their own bestiality toward blacks while others saw it as cause to promote more humane treatment for these supposedly lesser beings. Contrary to these European notions, blacks who were forcibly removed from their homeland had a sense of survival, both individually and collectively, which was fostered through the preservation of traditions. The narrative of Mary Prince, related by herself, exemplifies such attitudes.

It is important to note that Mary Prince's narrative came out of a resistance, particularly in the eighteenth century, that was inclusive of all members of the slave community. Women were active members of the resistance whether passively or in open revolt, but they were rarely acknowledged or recorded as participants. Barbara Bush, in her book *Slave Women in Caribbean Society 1650-1838*, explores the role of women in slave uprisings and notes their contributions often went unrecorded:

Thus a more balanced and realistic appraisal of the
woman's role in slave uprisings cannot be based solely on
biased contemporary accounts. Other important factors
must be examined; for instance the African cultural
heritage of the slave woman may have significantly
influenced her contribution to slave uprisings. [17]

As Bush relates here, regardless of the above-mentioned extenuating
factors, women in African culture were a part of the community's militia.
Olaudah Equiano (1745-1797), a freed Ibo, writes in his autobiography
that:

All are taught the use of these weapons; even our women
are warriors and march boldly out to fight along with the
men. There were many women as well as men on both
sides: among others my mother was there and armed with
a broad sword. [18]

Women of the Ibos, Yoruba, Dahomey, and other African communities
were renowned for their fierce warring spirit. [19] This tradition placed
women as active participants in, and initiators of, action against outside
aggression, whether European records recognized them during revolts or
not. The account of the uprising in Antigua in 1736, for instance, which
ended in the death of 47 slaves, only lists one woman. However, it notes
that slave women "by their Insolent behavior and Expressions had the
utter Extirpation of the White as much at heart, as the Men, and would
undoubtedly have done as much Mischief." [20]

This tradition of woman's resistance is also carried forward in the
folklore of Nanny stories. [21] Nanny was a Jamaican obeah woman who
not only fought with the Windward Maroons but exercised considerable
political influence in their activities. Her powerful influence, both as a
tactician and religious leader, was at the very least an aggravation for the
British. At the end of the First Maroon Wars in 1739, Nanny advised the
people to refuse a treaty offered by the British. After that time, however,
negotiations between the British and the Maroons focused on the group
leaders who were, more often than not, men. In Barbara Kopytoff's article
on "The Jamaican Maroon Political Organization," she states:

It was the headman to whom they looked, and they may
have expected him to perform duties that in the past fell to
her (Nanny); the fact that the British did not recognize a
religious leader may be the reason that none ever again
rose to Nanny's prominence and power. [22]

Nevertheless, maroon women as mothers, teachers, and warriors played
a vital role in maintaining a spirit of resistance. Many taught their children
contempt for the colonizers while openly displaying teeth and other
articles of slain soldiers. Philip Thicknesse's memoirs serve as a record
of the hostility he felt during his early days among the Jamaican Maroons:

> How maroon "pecananes" were bred to feel detestation
> towards white men. The children he came in contact with
> "could not refrain from striking their pointed fingers as
> they would knives" against his chest and shout "becara"
> [white man] at him in derision.[23]

Resistance often came in the form of covert action while still being
motivated by the need to aggressively respond to one's treatment.
Regarding women as active insurgents, Bush concludes:

> In the dual context of the African cultural heritage of the
> slave woman and her experience as a slave, it is far more
> credible to assume her active participation in African-led
> slave uprisings, than the passive non-involvement or more
> damning role as traitor implied by contemporary
> sources.[24]

The African-born instigators of slave uprisings in the mid-eighteenth
century served as forerunners of the Caribbean slave rebellions of the
nineteenth century. Although many of the rebellions were crushed, the
spirit and the continuation of resistance thrived in the attitude and behavior
of the generations that followed.

Punishment was a definite and deadly deterrent to resistance, but it
continued to surface in both domestic and political arenas. Ziggy
Alexander, in the preface to *The History of Mary Prince*, discusses
Caribbean women's role in these activities. She notes the comments of
one governmental official in Trinidad during 1823 who stated: "Female
slaves used to great effect that powerful instrument of attack and defence,
their tongues."[25] In Trinidad between 1824 and 1826, almost twice as
many women as men were officially punished: "Similarly, in Jamaica
during the years 1819 to 1835, although women were in the minority, they
accounted for nearly half the cases which came to court."[26] Slaves who
refused to work were brought to court as was the case of a female slave
named Industry. In 1831, she was presented before the magistrate in Port
Royal Jamaica for setting a bad example of not working. With such
resistance among women slaves, many overseers and owners saw the whip
as the only means of confronting the problem. The whip, utilized as a harsh
and destructive tool of submission, was an intricate part of women's lives.
When legislation against the whipping of black women was introduced in
1823 in Trinidad, the opinion of the slave owners was "that women slaves
were 'notoriously insolent' and only dealt with in some 'tolerable order'
through the fear of punishment."[27] No feelings for female weakness
hindered the use of the whip, which was used on pregnant women or on
the extremely aged or ill.

Despite these daunting conditions, complaints against whites brought
by slaves were not uncommon, and the numbers reported were only a
small portion of what may in fact have been entered. The records of one

administrator, Mr. Bennett from the House of Commons, are discussed in the June 23, 1825, *Anti-Slavery Monthly Reporter*:

> In transmitting these returns, [he] observes, that until the year 1819 he had kept no minutes of the complaints of slaves, but that from that time he had taken minutes of his examinations, but only in a few cases of his decision.[28]

The cases brought to court include one regarding Betto Douglas, a mulatto slave, age fifty-two, from St. Kitts, who in 1827 filed suit against her master for severe punishment. It seems he placed her in a one-foot stockade, day and night for a period of 6 months, because of her inability to pay a sum of three and a half dollars a month. She also complained that he withheld her manumission. Betto Douglas's concerns were denied since they were based on "such frivolous complaints," but it is significant that she raised them in the first place.[29] Another such case that had various hearings from 1819-1823 regarded nine black men who filed complaints against a Mrs. Saunders because of the lack of food and clothing.

> One man produced a bolt and shackles, with which the Negro women were often confined, the ancles (ankles) and wrists crossways, by which they are bent double; and says he was twice confined in that way. He and three others went on to complain of hunger and being forced to work on Sundays.... Negro Sam says: That his wife, named Adjuba was locked up lately in his mistress's house for six days, her allowance being only one plantain daily .[30]

Since the conferring of freedom required fees and taxes paid by the owner, and work stoppage on Sundays was not a law, all decisions lay in the hand of the mistress, therefore no sentencing resulted in this case. The most severe punishments for the owners might result in only a fine, even if the case regarded the death of a slave. Yet against such legal odds, slaves, when possible, did take their complaints to court, if to do no more than to damage the name of the owner.[31]

Mary Prince's open resistance to the physical and mental degradation to which she was subjected is an important aspect of her narrative which arises from the context of rebellion described above and is tied to the availability of family and community influences. Awareness of the linkage to histories that transcend the experiences of colonization and confront its degrading effects is important to understanding how slaves like Mary Prince found a way toward self-exploration and expression. The main focus of this discussion regarding Mary Prince's narrative is, in fact, that the process of identity formation as nurtured by collective histories, culture and family instilled in Mary a fearlessness in defending her rights as a human being.[32] We hear Mary's voice, not just within her narrative recounting her experiences but as her collectively inspired individual and immediate rejection of situations that she deemed reprehensible. Her resistance to many experiences is overt and offered at the time of abuse, placing her own sense of right against that of her master. Even after being flogged and finding no true safety by returning to her family, for instance, Mary asserts the truths of her humanity and speaks out seven times on her own behalf and on the behalf of others. It is Mary, furthermore, who initially intercedes for herself. While some forms of covert resistance among slaves consisted of stealing, dissembling, and arson, Mary moves beyond those responses to a more overt and politically aggressive stance. She progresses swiftly to a position of confrontation.

> He struck me so severely for this, that I at last defended myself, for I thought it was high time to do so. I told him I would not live longer with him, for he was a very indecent man—very spiteful; with no shame for his servants, no shame for his own flesh. (68)

Here we see Mary making shrewd use of the politics of British colonial society in her assault on the slaveholder's reputation. By refusing the moral condition of how her master lived, while not openly refuting the inhumanity of slavery, she could bring severe attention to her master as a moral and representative agent of British society. It was a situation in which the slaveholder would need to respond to abolitionists, the British reading community, and ultimately to religious authority. Thomas Pringle, the publisher of Prince's narrative, makes us aware of these issues in his statements regarding Mr. Wood, Captain I-- and his wife, and Mr. D--:

> [Mr Wood] appears to have exasperated [sic] his feelings of resentment towards the poor woman, to a degree which few people alive to the claims of common justice, not to speak of christianity or common humanity, could easily have anticipated. (87) These three people (Captain I--, his wife and Mr. D--) are now gone to answer to a far more awful tribunal than that of public opinion, for the deed of which their former bondwoman accuses them. (46)

The behavior of the slaveholder was often lacking in earthly consequences, but it could create difficulties in his moral and social acceptance by British society.

Since the influence of family and culture on her individual sense of self and her courage remains a key component to the narrative of Mary Prince, we need to examine specific elements of Mary's childhood. Mary Prince, who is estimated to have been born around 1788, was among the generation of slave children growing up during and after an openly rebellious period in the Caribbean.[33] In looking at the family situation of this generation of slaves, we see that the opportunity to learn from one's parentage became a key consideration in how these children were taught to survive. We cannot specifically determine what Mary Prince was taught, but she lived in a time when legal, religious, and individual resistance to slavery was active all around her. This rebellious ferment is evident when Mary tells us in her narrative a little about her childhood experiences and about her family. We find, for instance, that Mary had the benefit of both parents' sporadic but locatable presence. She knew that her mother spent part of her life as a domestic while in Bermuda and was a field worker on Turk's Island.[34] She also knew that her father was a sawyer.[35] With a structure that fostered tentative family communication and the omission of fathers' names on birth certificates, if any existed, Mary's family unit still managed to create a household of kinships. Although it was, in Barry Higman's terms from his study *Slave Population and Economy in Jamaica 1807-1834* "a truncated family," it nevertheless functioned as a base of support for Mary.[36]

Mary Prince's family, particularly her mother, is explicitly acknowledged in the narrative. Although it does not name her, it says that her mother was a house slave, a reference to Mary's early years when she was under the protection of her mother along with the children of Mr. Williams, her mother's owner, until the age of twelve. Mary's memory of her mother exists despite the traumatic rupture of their relationship when Mary and her siblings were sold upon the death of Mrs. Williams. She tells us that her mother accompanied them to the auction block "weeping for the loss of her children" and bemoaning her inability to protect them.[37] At this point in the narrative, we see Mary grappling with the vivid recall of her mother's powerlessness to prevent the sale of her children as well as that of her father's betrayal by returning Mary when she runs away from her new owner to rejoin her parents after a severe beating:

> I had run away to my mother; but mothers could only weep
> and mourn over their children, they could not save them
> from cruel masters-the whip, the rope, and cow-skin.(60)

Her victory lies not in finding refuge with her family but in understanding ultimately where the "protective" role of family ended and her own power began. Her own role as resister was reenforced by her success in forestalling a whipping on the day she was returned. Thus, through her own resistance and self-defense and not the protection of family, the girl of about thirteen assumed the role of active resister.

The final mention of Mary's mother is during their meeting at Turk's Island. Captain I--, the owner from whom she ran away, eventually sold Mary to Mr. D-- who was a part owner of some salt ponds on Turk's Island. The four-week voyage from Bermuda to Turk's Island was difficult for Mary Prince, and when her mother came to Turk's Island via the same route, she became quite ill and was out of her head for some time, illustrating the hardship of the voyage. Mary's mother worked on Turk's Island for some years accompanied by a four-year-old daughter but eventually returned to Bermuda long before Mary's departure. Mary does

not speak of the degree of contact between herself and her mother, but
there is no doubt that Mary loved her. We see this in a passage prior to
her departure to Turk's Island, and again once she finds out about her
mother's arrival:

> Oh the Buckra people who keep slaves think that black
> people are like chattel, without natural affection. But my
> heart tells me it is far otherwise. (61) [Mary says of her
> mother's arrival] I could scarcely believe them [the
> islanders' reports] for joy....

Nothing is mentioned about any further meetings between them, but we
do learn that Mary's mother dies in Bermuda after Mary goes to Antigua.
      Although Mary's relationship to her parents was seriously eroded by
the slave system, as is evidenced by the vague connection with her mother
while they were on Turk's Island together and the absence of any
connection with her father, we see that Mary's early years with them
strongly influenced her. These were the years when her sense of worth
and value were developed. She suffered a traumatic separation, but her
ability to cope and survive clearly came from the nurturance they were
able to provide, constrained as it was by the slave system. Mary, therefore,
not only knew what suffering she had to endure, but she also was able to
draw limits to that suffering when she needed to.
      There are two moments of resistance to her owner, Mr. D--, on Turk's
Island, that are worthy examples of Mary's adult strength, a strength that
could only have grown from her early family experience. One of these is
when Mary protects Mr. D--'s own daughter from a beating, on her return
to Bermuda after ten years on Turk's Island. Mary defies Mr. D--'s role
not only as father but as her master, for he has threatened to beat her as
well:

> I strove with all my strength to get her (Miss D-) away
> from him.... Then I said "Sir, this is not Turk's Island".
> He wanted to treat me the same in Bermuda as he had done
> in Turk's Island.(67)

Mary at this point defends another and calls attention to her owner's
responsibility for the way he treats her. She also rejects even the potential
of being abused as she had been on Turk's Island. Accusing one's master
is not the action of an individual who considers herself without defense
or some alternatives.
      The other instance of resistance is when Mary finally terminates her
time with Mr. D-- by telling him she will not stay after he strikes her for
not coming to wash his nude body. She defends her right to reject such
behavior in strong language:

> I told him I would not live longer with him, for he was a
> very indecent man—very spiteful; with no shame for his
> servants, no shame for his own flesh. (68)

Mary has put limits on the amount of injustice and indignity she will tolerate while recognizing that, unlike the time at Turk's Island, there were alternatives for her. It was one thing to work and work hard but quite another matter to be a servant to one that was "indecent and without shame." Mary's blatant rejection of Mr. D-- is not about labor, for as a slave work is what she *must* do. She rejects him because of his moral degradation and lack of common decency. Moira Ferguson in her introduction to the narrative concludes from her research that "This episode broaches that concealed area of Mary Prince's life taken up with sexual abuse and harassment."(9) It also is one of the only incidents that separates Mary's narrative from the male narratives which make no mention of sexuality.

In addition to the considerable influence of her familial legacy, we must not overlook the influences of the blacks on Turk's Island who may well have encouraged Mary's resistance to her treatment by Mr. D--. Ferguson, from her research, also informs us that:

> Even more importantly, talk of freedom abounded on the
> island for it was only 200 miles from San Domingo, a free
> republic after the successful revolution in 1791 by slaves
> led by Toussaint L'Ouverture and his allies. Slaves From
> Turk's Island frequently escaped to San Domingo.(9)

With such close proximity to a successful rebellion less than 30 years earlier and the collective planning that "frequent" escapes entail, it is likely that Mary knew something of oppositional activities. We can be relatively sure of this since a slave from Turk's Island felt secure in informing Mary of the destruction of a prayer shed by whites. Although we do not know what the role of the prayer shed actually was, it was obviously, by virtue of its destruction, a center of resistance and not sanctioned by the whites.

Moreover, Mary, like many slaves as in the forementioned example, made use of religion as a support for resistance. After her return to Bermuda, for instance, she highlights her visit to a Methodist meeting on a neighboring plantation. She tells us the prayers she heard at the meeting were "the first ones she understood," not necessarily the first ones she had heard or the first time she experienced spiritual togetherness. This is a significant word choice, for we know that the African religion of obeah was suppressed by whites on the island and that a leading citizen of Antigua, Sarah Gilbert, wrote that "obeahmen were once the terrors of estates."[38] Whatever Mary's connection with obeah or the prayer shed on Turk's Island, it is only after her stay there that she effected a move toward a religion that was sanctioned by the dominant culture and therefore available to her for community support.

Mary's shrewd use of religious authority would prove key in her penultimate rebellion from her fourth owner when she angrily leaves the Woods' household after being threatened for the fourth time with dismissal and proclaims her worth as a good worker, insisting on a moment to speak her piece:

> Stop before you take up this trunk, and hear what I have to say before these people .... I have done no wrong at all to my owners, neither here nor in the West Indies. I always worked very hard to please them both night and day; but there was no giving satisfaction, for my mistress could never be satisfied with reasonable service. I told my mistress I was sick, and yet she has ordered me out of doors. This is the fourth time; and now I am going out.(80)

It is this awareness of an opportunity to be heard and of her power in speaking in defence of herself that aided Mary in her decision to tell her story as "Related by Herself." (This addition to the title, "by Herself," which may or may not be seen as a source of authenticity, also attempts to demonstrate the abilities of a people thought incapable of such skills of communication.) Mary knew the extent of her opportunity as she knew the significance of her parting declaration to those within hearing at the Woods' residence.

Mary was able to seize the defining moment of autonomy during her departure from the Woods, in part because of her involvement with the Moravian church, which she joined in 1816 without the consent of her mistress. Her religious affiliation allowed her the spiritual support she needed to complement the ancestral and community resources that had been working in her life thus far. Mary's conversion to Moravianism suggests the influence of African culture, for African people held religion high as a source of their beliefs about themselves and the world around them.

> The life force of the Creator was thought to be present in all things, animate and inanimate. This force, "a kind of individualized fragment of the Supreme Being itself," continued to exist, even after the death of the individual. It continued, the African said, in a pure and perfect state which could influence the lives of living things.[39]

One explanation of Africans' willingness to accept the religion of the whites who enslaved them was the use of baptism, "the dip," as rebirth. In the African tradition water may have also been considered "a vehicle for reincarnation or a way to communicate with the other side."[40] Moravian missionaries who preceded other denominations to the Caribbean, were more flexible in addressing the cultural practices of the Africans than other religions that came to crush non-European behaviors.

> Operating in an institutional vacuum, the Moravian
> mission provided a place where slaves could meet and not
> feel slavish, while providing opportunities for talented and
> ambitious slaves—who were becoming so troublesome
> elsewhere. The Moravians confronted slave polygamy,
> which other sects attacked with the zeal of crusaders, in a
> restrained and practical manner.[41]

Once other denominations began to stream into the Caribbean, there were many revivals and conversions throughout the islands. Antigua counted "5,424 slave baptisms in the fifteen years between 1793 and 1808 or more than a third of the 13,278 converted during the Moravian's first fifty years in the island."[42] Although some benefitted from the initial teachings of the Moravians, many slaves shrewdly realized their usefulness to them. J.H. Buchner, a Moravian church historian and Jamaican missionary, states that:

> There is a shrewdness and sagacity on account of the
> deference and respect which they pay to the white man.
> But they are not slow in forming a pretty correct estimate
> of the man they have to deal with, and shaping their course
> accordingly.[43]

A casual visitor may not have been privy to such an observation, but Buchner recognized that the slave saw religion as an opportunity to "do what whites would not have them do, and know what others would not have them know."[44]

The Moravian religion was Mary's first choice, but her subsequent religious decisions illustrate the efficacious use she made of religious affiliation for her secular freedom. Because the German Moravian Church was not recognized by the English Church, Mary was baptized in the latter in 1817. She then married in 1826 within the Moravian Church as slave marriages were illegal in the English Church. There is another revealing chapter in Mary's religious life that occurred when she left the Woods while they were in England, ending over thirteen years of service, and sought refuge in the Moravian church. After this, aided by friends, she found employment with the Pringle family, who brought her story to the public. While employed by the Pringles, Mary was tutored in Methodist doctrines by Pringle's wife and their neighbor, a Methodist minister.[45] She attended church three times a day on Sundays, and it is evident that religion bolstered Mary's sense of herself as an empowered individual and provided legitimation for her efforts to direct her life.

Much of what Mary Prince tells in her narrative is tempered by religious and abolitionist goals, but Mary's unique voice can still be heard. There are passages recounting atrocities done to others as well as to Mary, for instance, that appear consistent with Mary's behavior toward exposing inhumanity and brutality in securing black people's freedom. At the end of the narrative, in fact, Mary claims her right to speak as coming from her experience of great suffering.

> Oh the horrors of slavery! — How the thought of it pains my heart! But the **truth** ought to be told of it; and what my eyes have seen, **I think it is my duty to relate; for few people in England know what slavery is.** I have been a slave — **I have felt** what a slave feels, and **I know** what a slave knows; and I would have all the good people in England to know it too, that they may break our chains, and **set us free.** (64) [emphasis added]

The authority of her own claims and her possession of truths regarding slavery are evident in her language and a emphatic use of "I."

Although Mary Prince's voice comes through powerfully in this and other ways, it is important to note the ways in which her narrative is shaped by the powerful white abolitionist who published it.[46] Thomas Pringle was not unresponsive to issues of justice and humanity in the treatment of blacks, but as an abolitionist and a Methodist, the corruption of the slaveholder's spirit by slavery was a campaign that he addressed with great emphasis. In his own comment on the narrative about the dehumanizing effects of slavery, for instance, he foregrounds slaveholders as victims of slavery themselves:.

> After a residence myself of six years, in a slave colony, I am inclined to doubt whether, as regarding *demoralizing* influence, the master is not even a greater object of compassion than his bondsman. (109)

Elsewhere he elaborates: "the general rule: the unquestionable tendency of the system is to vitiate the best tempers, and to harden the most feeling hearts."[47] What he does not address are the systematic and internalized racist attitudes that were often used to vindicate the guilty masters and diminish the doctrines of human rights that the so-called Christians so loudly professed.

We do see one instance where Mary categorically criticizes the behavior of whites in the narrative:

> Since I have been here I have often wondered how English people can go out into the West Indies and act in such a beastly manner. But when they go to the West Indies, they forget God and all feeling of shame, I think, since they can see and do such things. (83)

This is the only point, however, where Mary launches such an attack. Elsewhere she appears to have been restrained from any lengthy descriptions of slaveholders' marred character. A similar omission occurs when Mary notes the evil that her mistresses and masters do but not the pain and anguish she must have felt regarding those situations. When she is being sold from her mother, for instance, she says that whites are not all bad, only that "slavery hardens white people's hearts"(52). We are given vivid accounts of brutality but no interrogation of the humanity of the brutalizers. Even in the case of Mr. D-- whom she declared "indecent, spiteful and with no shame," (68) Mary is silent as to the "nature" of his indecency. It is evident that in spite of the power of Mary's narrative and the support of some whites, her voice was often silenced for, after all, she was still a black woman with little or no power and economic independence. The lack of evaluative statements regarding the perpetrators of these brutal deeds makes clear, as we have seen, the motive for their exclusion.

Regardless of the influences on and silences in *The History of Mary Prince, A West Indian Slave,* we clearly see the triumph of black female resistance to injustice. It is important also to recognize that resistance, even when supported by cultural and ancestral knowledge for the African, meant confronting the issue of silence as a tool for survival. The degree to which this affected Africans' opportunity to speak out in different situations of colonization and oppression is reflected in their public defenses of themselves and others. Narratives such as Frederick Douglass's used binary opposition by opposing two unrelated elements to create the presence and absence of some quality; Olaudah Equiano avoids emotional display in order to produce an unmanipulated and, thus, a natural response of emotion; and Harriet Jacobs, like Mary Prince, chose not to address directly the issue of sexual abuse.[48] These strategies appear to be conscious exclusions and not mandated constructs to be enforced, while other omissions seem dictated from spiritual concerns.

The History of Mary Prince allows for a broad exploration of individual and collective histories along with cultural, family, and religious influences for people of the African diaspora as they confront and resist oppression. It presents the evolution of one woman's identity, the fact that she had choices of expression and exploration, and the inevitable price for those choices that she as an enslaved African woman had to pay for self-preservation due to her exile from her mother and the motherland. It also demonstrates the central link between freedom for the individual and welfare of the community.[49] As Mary says in the narrative, "In telling my own sorrows, I cannot pass by those of my fellow-slaves for when I think of my own griefs, I remember theirs"(65).

Even though Mary Prince's is a Caribbean slave narrative, the rupture of her people that colonization propagated is a common bond of forced subjugation that people of the diaspora share. The ability to maintain and sustain histories, traditions, family guidance and protection was a function of the circumstances that geography presented as well as the repressive strategies of colonizers. In the diaspora, controlling strategies were effective in alienating Africans from one another to varying degrees, but they were met by the Africans' conscious adaptation of past knowledge to present circumstances in order to survive. Women, in particular, were cognizant of these adaptations for the sense of future generations was continually reinforced with the birth of each child or the responsibility for children in the community. Since men were often forced from the family units, their perspectives may have differed, but they were always recognized as necessary to family units as well. In spite of the fact that slavery tried to eliminate the traditions of the enslaved, slave resistance confronted the violation of slaves' humanity. The tools of survival, which encompassed family and personal histories, along with cultural traditions and participation of the community, served in varying degrees throughout the diaspora to help free the mind, spirit, and body from negative perspectives of self and the world for the African. It is this sense of identity as it emerges through oppression, which is continually replayed in works of the Diaspora from the slave narrative to autobiography, biography, and fiction. These works attest to the ability of the dispossessed to sort out the tools for survival that allow them to seek a kind of respect and dignity for their value and place as part of a universe much greater than the narrow world of unjust exploitation.

Chronology of Mary Prince or James,
Commonly Called Molly Wood
Self Realization through Kin and Culture
The History of Mary Prince, A West Indian Slave, Related by Herself

—   Born Brackish Pond - Bermuda
1788   Mother - House slave owned by Mr. Charles Myners
         Father - owned by Mr. Trimmingham, a shipbuilder at
         Crow Lane. Mary's father was trained as a sawyer.

—   Mr. Charles Myners died.
         Mary (an infant) and her mother were then sold to
         Captain Darrels. Captain Darrels gave Mary to his
         granddaughter, Betsy Williams.
         Betsy's parents were Captain and Mrs. Williams.
         Captain Williams was master of a vessel which traded
         to several places in America and the West Indies.

         Mary's mother took care of the Williams children,
         along with Mary, two brothers, and three sisters
         born to Mary's mother, while she was in Captain Williams'
         service.

1799   Mary was hired out at twelve years old to Mrs. Pruden,
         who lived five miles off in the adjoining parish. Mary's
         duties at Mrs. Pruden's were to nurse baby Daniel and to care
         for his sister Fanny and brother James. Fanny taught Mary
         letters and spelling.

—   Mrs. Williams died.
         Three months later, Mary Prince was brought back from
         Mrs. Pruden's and sold along with her other siblings. The
         fact that MP was originally given to Betsy Williams by her
         grandfather was ignored.

—   Mary was sold to Captain I.-- at Spanish Point.
         Mrs. I.-- was fierce and often used her fist to discipline.
         This was a terrible place for Mary, as she tells of how
         the slave girl Hetty was killed and how Mary herself was
         often stripped, hung by the wrist, and "licked" severely for
         minor offenses. She took matters into her own hands after
         one such incident and ran away to her mother and father.
         Mary was returned to Captain I.-- by her father, who asked
         mercy for his daughter and relief from such treatment that
         would cause Mary to run away and in turn be so brutally
         punished.

#1   I took courage and said that I could stand
the flogging no longer; that I was weary of
my life, and therefore I had run away to my
mother.... He did not flog me that day. (60)

Mary endured five more years of brutal treatment from
Captain I.--.

1805   Mary was sold to Mr. D--, owner of a salt pond.
Again Mary was often hung by the wrist, stripped, and
beaten with cow-skin. Mary saw her mother and sister
Rebecca briefly during her 10-year stay on Turk's Island.

During this time her father died in Bermuda.

—   Mary returned to Bermuda with Mr. D.--.

1815   Mary worked in Mr. D.--'s household waiting on his
daughters.

#2   I strove with all my strength to get her away
from him (Miss D.). Then I said, 'Sir, this is
not Turk's Island.... He wanted to treat me the
same in Bermuda as he had done in Turk's
Island. '(67)

#3   He struck me so severely for this, that I at last
defended myself, for I thought it was high time
to do so. I told him I would not live longer with
him, for he was a very indecent man —very
spiteful; with no shame for his servants, no shame
for his own flesh. (68) (Mr. D.-- had Mary wash
his naked body) (67)

Mary was hired out to do washing at a place called Cedar Hill.
While there, Mary heard a Mr. John Wood was going to
Antigua. She requested to go and work for Mr. Wood in
Antigua.

—   Mary accompanied Mr. Wood to Antigua and the town of
St. John. She was later purchased by Mr. and Mrs. Wood.

1816   Mary became very ill with rheumatism. She was treated very
badly by Mrs. Wood. Mary's mother died in Bermuda.

#4   I bore in silence a great deal of ill works: at
last my heart was quite full, and I told her

that she ought not to use me so: ...This was
a great affront.(70)

Mary was given a note to look for a new owner, but when
one offered to buy her, Mr. Wood said he did not really mean
to sell her.

Five years later, this same trick was played on Mary.
Mary tried to purchase her own freedom but was refused.

— Mary visited a Methodist Meeting at the Winthrop Plantation
during a Christmas the Woods spent at Date Hill.

1817 Mary was baptized August 30, 1817, in the English Church
by Rev. Mr. Curtin.

1826 Mary Prince married Daniel James, a black carpenter who
had purchased his freedom. As the marriage of a slave and
a free black was illegal in the English Church, Mary married
in a Moravian Chapel. When Mr. Wood found out, he was
vexed.

Again Mary asked to buy her freedom and was refused.

— Mary was taken to England by the Woods. Her rheumatism
made it difficult to do laundry and therefore was told to get out.
Mary stayed because she was a stranger to England and had
nowhere to go. She continued to work for the Woods, while
enduring great pain and being subjected to continual abuse.

1826 #5 I also said myself... since my mistress would
work me so hard, without compassion for my
rheumatism. (MP spoke up in her own behalf)
When the Woods heard this... (Mary spoke up
in her own behalf about her illness and her
treatment). (77)

1827 #6 My only fault was being sick, and therefore
unable to please my mistress ...and I told them
so... (78)

— After two to three months of being told to leave and
continued ill treatment, Mary Prince did leave the Wood
household. This ended thirteen years of servitude.

#7 Stop before you take up this trunk, and hear what
I have to say before these people....I told my

> mistress I was sick, and yet she has ordered me
> out of doors. This is the fourth time; and now
> I am going out. (80)

—   Aided by Mash (the shoe blacker), Mary went to the
      Moravian Missionaries for help. Mary stayed with Mash's
      family for many months until her health improved.

1828   Late November Mary went to the Anti-Slavery Society seeking
      assistance. She was referred to Mr. George Stephen, a lawyer.

—   Mary Prince spent her first Winter in England, aided by
      Quaker Ladies and other kind persons while doing some
      laundry jobs as her health improved.

—   Mr. and Mrs. Wood refused Mary Prince her freedom,
      even though offered large sums of money by the Anti-Slavery
      Society.

1829   Mary Prince went into the service of a Mr. and Mrs. Thomas
      Pringle, who were sympathetic to her plight and were advocates
      against the system of slavery. Mary was given religious
      instructions by the Pringles and parish clergy.

1831   *The History of Mary Prince, A West Indian Slave,*
      Related by Herself was published in London and Edinburgh,
      England, as a supplement by Thomas Pringle.

      #8   The horrors of slavery! - How the thought
            of it pains my heart! But the truth ought to
            be told of it; and what my eyes have seen, I
            think it is my duty to relate; for few people
            in England know what slavery is. I have been
            a slave - I have felt what a slave feels, and
            I know what a slave knows; and I would have
            all the good people in England to know it too,
            that they may break our chains, and set us free. (84)

1833   The Bill for the Abolition of Slavery passed through
      its critical second reading on August 28.

Notes

1. The usage of "Himself," or "Herself," as part of the slave narrative's aim is discussed in regard to Southern narratives by Henry Louis Gates, Jr., in the introduction of *The Slave's Narrative*, Charles T. Davis and Henry Louis Gates, Jr. (New York: Oxford University Press, 1985). Gates states, "Perhaps the most remarkable facet of the texts of the slaves in the South is the copious corpus of narratives that the black slave wrote 'Himself,' or 'Herself,' as the narratives subtitles attest. When, in the history of slavery, have the enslaved reflected upon his own enslavement by 'representing' its hideous contours through the spoken and the written arts? Representing the institution of slavery, in the sense of mimesis, implies indictment, but it also implies something of the representativeness of the slave narrator himself vis-a-vis his 'experience' of slavery as well as his relationship to other slaves. (xxiii).

2. Hazel V. Carby, *Reconstructing Womanhood: The Emergence of the Afro-American Woman Novelist* (New York: Oxford University Press, 1987), 61. Carby, while discussing the emergence of the black woman novelist, looks to the slave narrative as a literary convention that is reflected in the twentieth century's struggle for black liberation. She states that "The consequences of being a slave woman did not end with the abolition of slavery as an institution but haunted the texts of black women throughout the nineteenth century and into the twentieth. The transition from slave to free woman did not liberate the black heroine or the black woman from the political and ideological limits imposed on her sexuality."

3. Ronald A.T. Judy, *Dis-Forming the American Canon: African-Arabic Slave Narratives and the Vernacular* (Minneapolis: University of Minnesota Press, 1993), 85. Self-recognition, according to Judy, is a problematic process. For example, Judy explores Equaino's narrative as exemplary of the horror that is exacerbated by the slave's inability to forget his personal history before enslavement. Mary Prince's text is actually a revision of these two ideas, for even though her process toward identity is spurred to some degree by slavery, her ability to reject inhumanity is made possible by ancestral and community histories that encourage her *not* to forget but to consciously remember. Such histories or memories, both oral and written, are the basic components of "rememory" that is a key element in Toni Morrison's *Beloved*.

4. Carby, *Reconstructing*, 22. Carby notes that "It is necessary to historicize literary practices to be able to adequately consider the particular constraints in operation, for example, in the writing of a slave narrative by a man as opposed to a woman, constraints that were influenced by factors of race and gender and were inflected very differently in a diary by a Southern White woman. While acknowledging

that forms of racism and patriarchy are older than the economic system of slavery in the United States and the Caribbean, it is also possible to recognize the particular ways in which racism and black sexuality are articulated in the patriarchal system of the antebellum South."

5. Carole Boyce Davies "Writing Home: Gender and Heritage in the Works of Afro-Caribbean/American Women Writers," *Out of the Kumbla: Caribbean Women and Literature*, eds. Carole Boyce Davies and Elaine Savory Fido (Trenton, NJ: African World Press, Inc., 1994), 60.

6. Davies correctly notes a further discussion of sexual and societal politics in Barbara Christian's "Trajectories of Self Definition," *Conjuring: Black Women, Fiction, and Literary Tardition*, eds. Marjorie Pryse and Hortense J. Spiller (Bloomington: Indiana University Press, 1985), 233-248.

7. Jacqueline Jones, *Labor of Love, Labor of Sorrow: Black Women, Work, and the Family from Slavery to the Present* (New York: Vintage Books, 1995), 3-10.

8. In my research I refer to the Caribbean as consisting of Cuba, Hispanola, Jamaica, Puerto Rico, with a group of smaller islands such as Antigua and Santo Domingo.

9. Michael Mullin, *Africa in America: Slave Acculturation and Resistance in the American South and the British Caribbean*, 1736-1831 (Chicago: University of Chicago Press, 1994), 271.

10. Mullin, *Africa*, 45.

11. In the late 1730s maroons in the British Caribbean signed peace treaties. Michael Mullin in *Africa in America* denotes politically sanctioned groups of Maroons with capitalization. These treaties in my chapter are also designated by the capitalization in accordance with Mullin's model.

12. Mullin, *Africa*, 46.

13. Mullin, *Africa*, 45.

14. Sidney W. Mintz, *Caribbean Transformations* (Chicago: Aldine Press, 1974), 31.

15. Mintz, *Caribbean*, 33.

16. Quoted in Eric Williams, *Capitalism and Slavery* (Chapel Hill: University of North Carolina Press, 1994), 180.

17. Bush also notes that women were often in the majority when slave populations were assessed. Recognizing the participation of women adds to our sense of the intensity of resistance by the sheer numbers of women present. Barbara Bush, *Slave Women in Caribbean Society, 1650-1838* (Bloomington: University of Indiana Press, 1990), 67.

18. Olaudah Equaino, or, Gustavus Vassa the African, *Equaino's Travels* (Portsmouth: Heinemann Press, 1969), 9-10.

19. Women in African society participated in all capacities that preserved the continuance of the community. See Denise Paulme, ed., *Women in Tropical Africa* (Berkeley: University of California Press, 1963); Maria Rosa Cutrufelli, trans., Nicolas Romano, *Women of Africa: Roots of Oppression* (London: Zed Press, 1983); and Rosalyn Terborg-Penn, Sharon Harley, Andrea Benton Rushing, eds., *Women in Africa and the African Diaspora* (Washington, DC: Howard University Press, 1987).

20. Barry D. Gaspar, "The Antigua Slave Conspiracy of 1736," *William and Mary Quarterly* 35:2 (April 1978), 308-323.

21. "Nanny" survives in many stories about escape and is carried over in African American folktales in the Auny Nancy, Ann Nancy, Annancy tales. See Roger D. Abrahams, ed., *Afro-American Folktales: Stories from Black Traditions in the New World* (New York: Pantheon Books, 1985), 19-24; and Bruce R. Beckley, *Joel Chandler Harris* (Athens: University of Georgia Press, 1987).

22. Barbara Kopytoff, "Jamaican Maroon Political Organization: The Effects of the Treaties," *Social and Economic Studies* 25 (June 1976), 101-120.

23. Philip Thicknesse, *Memoirs and Anecdotes of P. Thicknesse* (London: Printed for the Author 1788-91), 2 vols.

24. Bush, *Slave*, 73.

25. *The History of Mary Prince, A West Indian Slave Related by Herself* (Ann Arbor: University of Michigan Press, 1993), xi. All page numbers listed in this chapter are from this edition of the text.

26. *Prince*, xi.

27. Bush, *Slave*, 42.

28. *Anti-Slavery Monthly Reporter* was published in London from 1825-1833. It included numerous court cases involving slaves, on-going debates and issues regarding slavery, and the minutes from Anti-Slavery society meetings. (Resource: John Rylands University Library of Manchester, Anti-Slavery Collection)

29. *Anti-Slavery Monthly Reporter*, #25, 1827. "Case of Betto Douglas, A St. Kitts Slave," Dated June 1827 Vol. I, No. ii, 1-7.

30. *Anti-Slavery Monthly Reporter*, #5, 1825. "BERNICE—Fiscal's Returns, printed by order of the House of Commons," 23rd June, 1825.

31. It is important not to forget that justice and humane treatment were always the goals of the slaves and those who supported them in seeking legal actions. This is exemplified when any case in the *Anti-Slavery*

Reporter is discussed and the verdicts and their rationale challenged as justice. Regarding the "Case of Betto Douglas, A St. Kitts Slave—United States—Slave Population of the West Indies," the following comments were made: "Can anything show more strongly than this contrast, which any Englishman may realize to himself, the state of feeling which exists in Colonial communities as to all that affects the wretched slave when his claims are brought into competition with the authority or the pride of interests of the master or manager; or when a black or brown complexion, nay, when even a single tinge of African blood stands opposed, before a jury of planters, to the unlimited power, and the not-to-be-questioned superiority of the white?" (June 1827), 6-7.

32. Sandra Pouchet Paquet, "The Heartbeat of a West Indian Slave: *The History of Mary Prince*," *African American Review* (Spring 1992), 26.1, 131-146. Paquet in her review of the narrative says that "Mary Prince reproduces and revises images of the heart in an elaborate pattern of signification that reflects the myriad voices and values of the text as managed elements of her own voice." I maintain that ancestry and memory are the sources of these images which nurture the base from which resistance springs. Paquet is correct in stating "The physical and psychological torture of a lifetime leaves her (Mary Prince) childless, crippled with arthritis, blind, and in exile. But her embattled body is the vessel of a defiant tribal spirit of resistance that she refashions in memory and characterizes as heart. The fashioning of this trope as a center of value in her epic tale of bondage and deliverance is her own act of creative memory; its origins are oral and familial and illuminate the oral beginnings of West Indian culture in a community under seige." (143)

33. It is footnoted in Mary Prince's narrative that she was forty-two when the history was given. From this is derived her possible birth date and the issues of self-realization that evolve as she matures into a woman.

34. Bush, *Slave*, 36 and 38. The majority of work in the Caribbean took place in the field, and women in the Caribbean slave society were either field hands or domestics. Although planters professed a greater need for men than women, "modern researchers have found that planters may have exaggerated the adverse sex ratio to play down the exploitation of women slaves as field hands. The majority of women, however, remained working in the fields, in harsh conditions and maintained by their owners at a bare subsistence level. Demographics analysis by Higman confirms the dominance of women in field gangs after 1800."

35. Bush, *Slave*, 34. Black men like Mary's father were owned because of their talent in a certain trade: "Within this complex occupational stratification of slaves, the position of the woman slave was generally less favorable than that of her male counterpart."

36. Barry Higman, *Slave Population and Economy in Jamaica 1807-1834* (New York: Cambridge University Press, 1976), 75-93. "The simple family household (here defined as simple nuclear units) and what might be described as truncated nuclear families (man and wife, father and children, mother and children) account for the greater part of the slave family."

37. Brenda F. Berrian, "Claiming An Identity: Caribbean Women Writers in English," *Journal of Black Studies* (December 1994), 25.2, 200-216. Berrian discusses the need of a maternal presence in the formation of female identity and how its absence has an effect on the establishing of that identity. Berrian uses Mary Prince's narrative as the literary example of an identity nurtured by a maternal presence. "Several English-speaking Caribbean women writers stress the importance of knowing one's history. The interrelationship leads to the formation of female identity. All write about mothers as vehicles of culture and history. Once this function is removed from biological mothers, the daughters become confused about their history and place in it."

38. Mullin, Africa, 204.

39. Lerone Bennett, Jr., *Before the Mayflower: A History of Black America*, 5th ed. (New York: Penguin Books, 1982), 24.

40. Mullin, Africa, 204.

41. Mullin, Africa, 243-45.

42. Mullin, Africa, 249.

43. Mullin, Africa, 245.

44. Mullin, Africa, 204.

45. Kari J. Winter, *Subjects of Slavery, Agents of Change: Women and Power in Gothic Novels and Slave Narratives, 1790-1865* (Athens: The University of Georgia Press, 1992), 85-110. Winter explores the relationship between white women and Mary Prince as one of common bondage as well as that of victim and victimizer.

46. Jane Meiring, *Thomas Pringle: His Life and Times* (Capetown: A.A. Balkema, 1968).

47. There are several appendices to the *History of Mary Prince* in which Pringle makes comments about the conduct of Mary and his own attitude about slavery and the truth of Mary's narrative.

48. Henry Louis Gates, Jr., *Figures in Black: Words, Signs, and the "Racial" Self* (New York: Oxford University Press, 1987), 87. Gates, in discussing the *Narrative of the Life of Frederick Douglass, an American Slave, Written by Himself,* comments on Douglass's rhetorical strategy:"In the act of interpretation, we establish a sign relationship between the description and a meaning. The relations most crucial to

structural analysis are functional binary oppositions." Jean Fagan Yellin states that, "Presenting herself as a heroic slave mother, Jacobs's narrator includes clear detail, uses straightforward language, and when addressing the reader directly, utilizes standard abolitionist rhetoric to lament the inadequacy of her descriptions of slavery and to urge her audience to involve themselves in antislavery efforts. But she treats her sexual experiences obliquely, and when addressing the reader concerning her sexual behavior, pleads for forgiveness in the overwrought style of popular fiction." Jean Fagan Yellin, ed., *Incidents in the Life of a Slave Girl Written by Herself* (Cambridge: Harvard University Press, 1987), xiv.

49. Joanne M. Braxton, *Black Women Writing Autobiography: A Tradition Within a Tradition* (Philadelphia: Temple University Press, 1989), 40. Braxton comments on how the "Narratives of free women and former slave women tend to differ from those of fugitives in that the writing of autobiography stands as a literary experience wherein slavery has less importance as a theme. The author is involved in creating a public persona, but the impulse to write is less overtly political because the need to raise public opinion against slavery has diminished. While these works lack the emotional confessional quality of such fugitive narratives as *The Narrative of Frederick Douglass* and *Incidents in the Life of a Slave Girl*, they sustain the themes of family and survival, and they reflect a movement toward self-sufficiency and self-expression, and toward an intelligent and self-conscious sensibility that seeks to satisfy its own needs."

CHAPTER 3

Toni Morrison's *Beloved*

Evolving Identities from Slavery to Freedom

Toni Morrison's novel, *Beloved*, explores a tug-of-war between life and death and challenges her characters to find the dignity and meaning that may exist in both. Because these characters grapple with Emancipation in post-Civil War America, it is imperative to examine the issues in this novel that arise out of slavery in terms of their impact on the individual and the community in *Beloved*. Through such an explication, a reader can get a sense of how slaves' self-identification had been repressed, devalued, and distorted by slavery's disregard for the human beings it defiled. Our exploration does not end here, for we are able to see in the novel an evolution of characters' identities through the process of interaction of collective and individual memories. It is through a reconstruction of personal and community histories and ancestral reclamation whereby all of the characters move on a continuum from a repressive slave perspective to an open, accepting, free perspective of self and environment. Morrison focuses primarily on the time period just after Emancipation so that a reclamation of memory and the reconstruction of fractured lives may be seen as a possible way for African Americans to free themselves figuratively and literally from slavery and to engage survival strategies that eliminate emotional and physical repression of the self. Morrison has recreated an historical moment that captures the complexities and difficulties of reclaiming self after slavery with its pernicious legacy.

To appreciate fully what the novel attempts, it is useful to understand the varying impacts of slavery on each individual and his or her community. The characters in *Beloved* are representative of slavery's emotional damage in post-Civil War America while their struggles to heal form a central theme for Morrison. Fundamental to the characters' sense of self is the dehumanization they undergo as slaves. Systematic degradation, as a key element in justifying control and ownership by whites, resulted in blacks being brutalized and exploited on every level. To deter self-defense by slaves, white oppressors implemented strategies to inhibit aggression from or vengeance by black men and women for the atrocities inflicted upon them.[1] The result was that responses considered natural under the circumstances such as physical acts of assertiveness and angry words became acts punishable by death. Slavery, in effect, deprived blacks of their right to a personality.[2] Lawrence N. Houston, in researching the psychology of the black experience, notes in his work, "Frustration and Adjustment," how these repressive strategies affected the African American:

> The result is that in spite of much inner turmoil, the individual presents a continuous facade of serenity. That this facade includes the suppression and repression of all emotions, including love, may have critical ramifications regarding not only Black-White relations but also Black male- female relationships.[3]

Houston describes the restriction and suppression of emotion through enforced catastrophic disruption of lives. The systematic selling of family members, rape and exploitation of black women, "studding" of black males, as well as open humiliation, brutality, and other dehumanizing acts of physical and cultural genocide were the weapons of control. They greatly affected the individual and collective interaction of black people with each other. Roberta Rubenstein in her essay "Pariahs and Community" comments on the damaging effects of slavery:

> The boundaries that circumscribe black people of both genders are not only the prejudices and restrictions that bar their entry into the mainstream, but the psychological ones they internalize as they develop in a social structure that historically has excluded them.[4]

Boundaries, Rubenstein correctly notes, for both genders were not just external ones but restrictions that affected the African Americans' attitude about themselves and their place in society.

   In spite of repressive strategies that left deep scars, resistance thrived as a necessary and real ingredient of slave life, but resistance, as we understand it today, was in many ways disguised. The relationship between disguise which conceals and resistance which carries a clear intent will be important in understanding the novel's central act of infanticide.[5] Eugene Genovese in his book *Roll, Jordan, Roll* discusses this complex notion of resistance:

> The slaves' response to paternalism and their imaginative creation of a partially autonomous religion provided a record of simultaneous accommodation and resistance to slavery. Accommodation itself breathed a critical spirit

> and disguised subversive actions, and often embraced its
> apparent opposite--resistance .... Stark physical resistance
> did not represent a sharp break with the process of
> accommodation except in its most extreme forms--running
> away to freedom and insurrection.[6]

Genovese goes on to talk about resistance as both actively political
(insurrection and escape) and passively political (stealing, lying,
dissembling, shirking work, murder, infanticide, suicide, and arson).

Angela Davis in her article, "Reflections on the Black Woman's Role
in the Community of Slaves," details the crucial role played by black
women in the survival of the slave community and its resistance to white
control:

> The consciousness of their [black women's] oppression,
> and the conscious thrust towards its abolition could not
> have been sustained without impetus from the community
> they pulled together, through the sheer force of their own
> strength.[7]

It is this resistance to domination that made black women such an effective
force in avoiding cultural and even physical annihilation. There are
numerous accounts found in the written records of slaveholders, such as
diaries and letters as well as magazines and newspapers, that recount the
resistance of women slaves to a system that created lives of unceasing
misery.

One such story is that of Margaret Garner recorded in *The American
Baptist* in 1856, the historical antecedent of Toni Morrison's *Beloved.*[8]
Garner's story is one we confront, as did Morrison, in seeking to reclaim
meaningful experiences from the African American past. She was
compiling material for *The Black Book*, a collection of memorabilia from
the seventeenth, eighteenth, and the nineteenth centuries, when she found
the account of Margaret Garner's story. It tells of a young slave woman,
twenty-five years of age, who attempted to kill all her children rather than
have them taken back into slavery. Garner was able to take the life of only
one of her children before she was captured. The misery the children
would suffer was known all too well by their mother during her life as a
slave, and Morrison comments on this knowledge by saying, "A woman
loved something other than herself so much, she had placed all of the value
of her life in something outside herself."[9] Slavery, in denying Margaret
Garner possession of her own life or that of her children, provoked her act
of infanticide, for death allowed her to take control of a situation in which
she had been deemed powerless.[10] Garner's compelling belief that her
only viable option was death empowered her with a resolve and control
that enabled her to take the life of her child.

In the 1856 newspaper account of the incident, "A Visit to the Slave
Mother Who Killed Her Child," Margaret Garner is quoted as saying: "I

was as cool as I now am."[11] Further on in the interview, she is asked if she had been "excited almost to madness when she committed the act."[12] Here we see Garner's inquisitors insisting on madness as her motivation, for their rejection of open resistance causes them to code her behavior as madness and murder.[13] Their presumption of madness reflected whites' questioning the ability of blacks to respond rationally to an intolerable situation. Rather than accepting Garner's act as a desperate yet rational response, many whites viewed it as a further example of blacks' lack of humanity. Only by taking this story back to the community, Morrison implies by creating her novel around this incident where it is connected to the experiences of other blacks, can this tragedy be reclaimed as female revolt. It is in this framework that one recognizes Garner was not "excited to madness," but that her reality was a kind of madness in itself. Garner's deliberate engagement of this madness allowed her to take control and, in fact, not lose her mind. Margaret Garner confronted the boundaries of her slave life as being unnatural or, in essence, an existence of bondage and misery enforced by white men. In order to preserve some aspect of physical and mental self-respect, which she had every right to claim, she wielded the one weapon slaveholders could not take away—death. Toni Morrison comments on this view of Garner's "mad act" in a 1988 interview about *Beloved*, where she validates:

> Certain kinds of dissolution, the loss of and the need to reconstruct certain kinds of stability. Certain kinds of madness, deliberately going mad in order, as one of the characters says in the book, "not to lose your mind."[14]

Morrison's positive definition of "madness" provides a way to step out on a limb, farther than the constructed parameters allow, in order to free oneself from the control of slavery. For some, like Margaret Garner, it is on the margins of madness that true sanity and identity may be found.

To appreciate the significance of Morrison's fictional representation of Margaret Garner, we need to be cognizant of Morrison's definition of madness and the complex relationship slave women had with their children. While children were perceived as a blessing and sign of hope to the slave community, they were at the same time vulnerable to the abuse of slaveholders. The female slave, therefore, bore the added responsibility to her conscience of bringing a life into a system that had no respect for that life. The fate of all the children a slave woman conceived lay heavily on her heart, but the female children, in particular, were subject to rape and sexual exploitation by their white slaveowners in addition to the numerous other physical and mental abuses all slaves endured.[15] Many women responded to this treatment by developing ways to abort pregnancies with herbs and potions. Recipes had been passed down from woman to woman, generation to generation, for those fortunate enough to have access to them. One historical incident testifies to this practice in that

a slave master during a period of twenty-five years was only able to sire
two children. He finally discovered that an old slave woman had supplied
medicines over the years to abort the pregnancies.[16] Several women in
Beloved speak to these historical realities and of their painful experiences
regarding pregnancies and the children they produced. For instance Ella,
a black woman from Cincinnati who had suffered many wrongs in her life,
gave birth to a "hairy white thing" that she refused to nurse. Baby Suggs,
Sethe's mother-in-law, tried to keep her children with her, but the game
of checkers that was played with slaves' lives through broken promises
and tricks proved to be lies. After being tricked for the third time, Baby
Suggs gives up:

> That child she could not love and the rest she would not.
> "God take what He would," she said. And He did, and He
> did.

A slave woman had few options, but faith and hope kept many women
and their children alive while overwhelming rage against slavery and a
desire to control one's own body resulted in abortions and infanticide. In
addition, many who witnessed the demise of their families and kin lost
their psychological buffer against slavery and survived by "loving small"
or in many cases by not loving at all.[17]

The pain that slavery caused in the process of slaves making
emotional commitments to each other forced many to "protect yourself
and love small" (162), if at all. Slavery had in fact created an expected
epitaph in loving others, for, more often than not, separation, loss, and/or
death were imminent. This risk was accompanied by a constant misery in
everyday life that was determined by the meanness and the variations of
treatment by one's masters.[18] We see for instance in *Beloved* that Sethe
while at Sweet Home knew of both kindness and meanness. With Garner,
a name that recalls the novel's historical subject, as her master when she
first came to Sweet Home, Sethe was not preyed upon sexually nor used
as a breeder of more slaves. She worked hard and was eventually allowed
to call herself wife to Halle, one of the five young male slaves on the
ironically named Sweet Home plantation. Out of this union Sethe had four
children and an extended family through Baby Suggs, Halle's mother.
Halle also during this period was allowed to hire himself out and buy his
mother's, Baby Suggs, freedom while Garner was master. This period of
relative safety was quickly ended, however, by the death of Garner:

> How 'bout that? Everything rested on Garner being alive.
> Without his life each of theirs fell to pieces. Now ain't that
> slavery or what is it? (220)

Life with Garner had at least allowed some refuge from abuse and the
day-to-day misery of slave life, but with the arrival of Schoolteacher as
master after Garner's death, this no longer was the case.

Understanding the role that the slaves played on a plantation makes the nature of home life or even the concept of home under slavery problematic and thus recognizable as a key subject in the novel. Where you were from, as established by your bondage, was only a place. A real home, in contrast, was the familiarity of being with and locating those for whom you cared, which was often an impossibility. Slave men were often confronted with the invasion of their homes by the rape and exploitation of their mothers, wives and lovers and separation from family members. The defiling of their homes and the rejection of their sense of manhood created emotional hurdles that many men, let alone the families themselves, could not get over.[19] Halle was among those who were confronted with their homes being defiled with the arrival of Schoolteacher. Schoolteacher brought to Sweet Home plantation abuse both literally and figuratively, which made freedom and escape more and more a risk to be considered by Halle, Sethe, and other slaves at Sweet Home. Life for them had become "unbearable."

Sethe, who had no fears of abuse or rape from whites on the plantation during Garner's time, became easy prey for Schoolteacher's nephews, who held Sethe down, beat her, and took the breast milk that was for her baby.[20] This treatment of Sethe, being milked and whipped like an animal, was a blatant rejection of her humanity and a confirmation of the slaveholders' disregard for her life. Halle, horrified after witnessing the brutal taking of Sethe's breast milk, lost his sense of self and reality. Because of Halle's success in buying his mother's freedom, he had considered himself a man both within and outside of the world of Garner, his first master. It was Halle's willingness to accept Garner's image of himself as a black man and his inability to recognize the dangers that existed outside the planation that caused his mind to shut down in escape from the truth of both these images. Halle's perspective regarding his manhood, the "wonderful lie" (221), once destroyed with the rupture of his family, left him caught between two worlds, neither of which he could accept. In the case of Halle, knowledge demanded that he face the true realities of slavery, but he could not. For Halle and the slaves at Sweet Home plantation, Schoolteacher epitomized and perpetuated the mean-spiritedness of slavery which relegated them as property on the Sweet Home plantation: "One step off that ground and they were trespassers among the human race"(125).[21] For a slave any sense of a true home became risky and seldom realized.

Once freedom became a legal right with the Emancipation Proclamation and the Fourteenth Amendment, blacks had to address a new perspective of themselves and family. The techniques of resistance and survival that slaves used to protect and buffer themselves from the atrocities of slavery had to be redirected and transformed to meet this new right of self-ownership. With Reconstruction came a time of great political reshaping of the American system in which blacks lived, while

Emancipation initiated the time when blacks had to reconstruct their sense of self and the rights and responsibilities that went with it.[22] Blacks had to rethink survival and relationships as they struggled to understand self-love and embraced the fact that "You your best thing"(273). The right to one's own body and life was something that most Blacks had not experienced. The commodification of one's body and one's life during slavery meant that body and life were not often loved because they were not often perceived as the possession of the individual. Only the soul, in its intangible presence, was rightfully claimed.

To reconstruct the image of self as the loving caretaker of both one's physical and emotional being was not so easily achieved. Personal worth and possessions took on meanings not of economic equations enforced by law, but of self-actualization manifested in loving oneself and others like oneself. It was freedom that removed limits and allowed one to choose and to affect the life that one lead. It allowed one to see value and possibilities in one's own ability, instead of pinning one's hope on the efforts of others.[23] This change in perspective became a difficult task for many blacks, as slavery had placed much pain within the lives of most. This pain, which resulted from the loss of loved ones, family members and kin, made freedom for many a way to affect the lives of those left who were dear to them. This was particularly true for black women who had seen chaos inflicted on their households through the callousness of slavery. In *Labor of Love, Labor of Sorrow*, Jacqueline Jones asserts that:

> For most black women, then, freedom had very little to do with individual opportunity or independence in the modern sense. Rather freedom had meaning primarily in a family context. Only at home could they exercise considerable control over their own lives and those of their husbands and children and impose a semblance of order on the physical world.[24]

It was through the natural and legal right to embrace others and establish relationships and families that blacks were able to move forward to a freer and more open perspective of their evolving world.

The reconstruction of family is a key element in *Beloved* and it is important that we use the slaves' definition of family, for survival was a function of many working together. Family consisted of those whom you loved and cared for, and for blacks both during and after slavery this would extend itself to the black community at large. There were common denominators of suffering that transcended lineage and caused people to act as a unified front. The novel illustrates what is involved in reconstructing family, home, individual autonomy, and community wholeness, for in it memory plays a key role in the reclamation of what slavery tried to annihilate. Undoubtedly, the novel suggests, in coming to terms with one's *whole* being, memory for the ex-slave encompasses painful experiences that have to be acknowledged before one can move past them. Such memories of pain are not necessarily to be "passed on" but validated as experiences that one has survived. In the novel, memory is further conceived of as "rememory--Some things you forget. Other things you never do" (36), that moves you toward those people who have lived a similar experience. One may well confront rememories that belong to others:

> It's when you bump into a rememory that belongs to somebody else. The picture is still there and what's more, if you go there--you who never was there--if you go there and stand in the place where it was, it will happen again; it will be there for you, waiting for you.(36)[25]

This confrontation with rememory is presented as leading one toward a collective experience which would remove individual isolation and promote healing.

Morrison's keen attention to the importance of memory or rememory stems from the historical reality that slave culture was based on an oral society, further reinforced by laws forbidding literacy to slaves. In the case of Margaret Garner, her story of suffering and infanticide was available to the white reading public but not to many blacks, since for them reading was illegal. Her story was separated from the slave community even while representing it. It is in the community of oral histories, in contrast, that such stories are passed down. This recall may encompass many voices and much pain, but it provides connection to the experiences of a people and the plight of the individual.

If one considers the role of the oral historian, the griot, in African culture, we see why oral history is a necessary part of reclamation in the African American experience. Cultural values based on remembering were important for the African community and were not taken lightly. Experiences collected about the community and dispersed by the griot, represented *their* past, *their* story as they lived it, which reflected *their* sense of the world and *their* condition in relationship to it. It is through memory of ancestors in particular, who provide a connectedness among these experiences, that the individual is then able to move forward once he or she has acknowledged the past. It is also through this awareness of one's past that the individual is empowered by one's own identity and thus able to move out into the community. In recognizing ancestry as a link to the reconstruction of self, Toni Morrison says in "Rootedness: The Ancestor as Foundation" that in African American writing, "these ancestors are not just parents, they are sort of timeless people whose relationships to the characters are benevolent, instructive, and protective, and they provide a certain kind of wisdom."[26] They operate as the instructional past, guidance for the present, and foundation of the future. This dependence on memory alone made things remembered and things forgotten even more important in reclaiming self for they served as building blocks in constructing individual and collective identities.[27]

The oral memories and histories that are hidden within the written erasure of blacks are opened to the reader of *Beloved* as the narrative style allows those histories to have a voice. It is the sharing of stories between the characters, in fact, that recreates this history. Like Paul D, their memories and rememories were "one by one into the tobacco tin lodged in his chest."(113) In order to reconstruct their personalities, characters like Sethe and Paul D have to reclaim those memories not only for their own healing, but for the sake of their families so that knowledge of survival is gained even if the story itself goes unwritten. For the characters, then, the process of rememory challenges the continued usefulness of those silences which were adopted to protect the community under slavery.

The central survival story told in the novel is that of a motherless child, Beloved, the young woman who arrives at # 124 out of nowhere, separated from her mother and taken from her homeland while still a child.[28] After losing her mother, we discover, she was locked away and used as a concubine by a white man in a neighboring town. Her sexuality and what sense of self she possessed were assaulted by the white man's disrespect for her body, her womanhood, and her humanity. "Folks say he had her in there since she was a pup. Well, now she's a bitch"(235). As a motherless child abused by a white man, Beloved is representative of the exploitation that slave women as a whole felt. Some slave women were able to aid each other when confronted with sexual exploitation, but Beloved was not so fortunate. For her, in the absence of community, there was only confusion.

We first meet Beloved as she walks out of a local stream fully dressed. We come to understand from her disjointed past, later on in the novel, that she entered the water seeking to embrace the reflection of a familiar face known to her as her mother, but in truth it was the reflection of herself that had aged in isolation as the concubine of her captor.

> she is the laugh I am the laugher I see her face which is
> mine it is the face that was going to smile at me in the place
> where we crouched now she is going to her face comes
> through the water ... she is chewing and swallowing I
> have to have my face I go in ... I am gone now I am her
> face ... I want to be the two of us I want to join (212-13).

After entering the water to join with the face of her mother that calls to her, Beloved finds she is gone. She can not embrace her mother, so again she is lost. Beloved exits the water still seeking refuge from the mental and physical isolation of being unloved and homeless:

> I come out of blue water ... I need to find a place to be ...
> I am not dead I am not there is a house ... Sethe sees me
> see her and I see the smile ... it is the face I lost she is my
> face smiling at me (213).

Once passing through the water as guided by the reflection of her own face, Beloved finds Sethe, and Beloved claims her as the maternal presence needed to recreate herself as a black female person with a history.

In the process of reconstructing self that is invoked with the meeting of Sethe and Beloved, memories which existed silent and undefined had to be reclaimed and confronted. Significantly, what we know of Beloved, the young woman, comes through that experience of reclamation or rememory. Beloved flashes back to bits and pieces of a time when she was trapped in the hold of a slave ship. This rememory of the Middle Passage is invoked just as it was experienced, through the understanding of a child, disconnected from the familiarity of home and the protection of her mother:

> there will never be a time when I am not crouching and
> watching others who are crouching too ... daylight comes
> through the cracks ...I am not big ... small rats do not wait
> for us to sleep... he is trying hard to leave his body... there
> is no room to tremble so he is not able to die... those able
> to die are in a pile... a hot thing ... the woman is there with
> the face I want the face that is mine... the woman with my
> face is in the sea a hot thing (211)

As a child of the Middle Passage, Beloved speaks of pain and loss and whispers of those things unspeakable and partly forgotten. From the pieces of her story comes recognition as she wrests meaning out of mysterious incantations such as "I AM BELOVED and she is mine" (210). "She" is that part of herself that is lost, and it is "she" who would make Beloved whole. "She smiles at me and it is my own face smiling" (214). We come to understand that it is the bonding of mother and daughter that makes each face one and the same. For Beloved the young woman, the true evolution of the relationship between mother and daughter was not hers to claim except through rememory of a collective rupture from mother Africa. With the presence of Sethe, the potential of Beloved coming to terms with her past and her whole being is made possible. The knowledge of this rememory makes Beloved possessive of her time with Sethe. Eventually this possessiveness turns to anger as Beloved blames the loss of this relationship on her mother whom she perceives Sethe to be.

> But it was Beloved who made the demands. Anything she
> wanted she got, and when Sethe ran out of things to give,
> Beloved invented desire. She wanted Sethe's company for
> hours ... Then the mood changed and arguments began.
> Beloved accused her of leaving her behind. Of not being

> nice to her, not smiling at her. She said they were the same,
> had the same face, how could she have left her? (240-41)

After rememory and the past have been reclaimed and confronted, the rupture of the mother-daughter relationship comes, not by force as was the case under slavery but by choice after Beloved had taken all she could from Sethe to recreate herself. Since Beloved remained inside the house, #124, and apart from the community of Cincinnati, she leaves with a clearer sense of her past but still disjointed from any sense of family and community.

The arrival of Beloved at #124 produced in Sethe a similar need to explain the past. For Sethe this meeting was the opportunity to explain her act of infanticide to one she perceived as her baby daughter reincarnated. It was imperative to Sethe that she share her rememories of slavery so that her child would know that her death was about love and freedom and not madness and selfishness. Only through sharing these memories could her baby know the pain and circumstance of her own life as a slave, a life that her child was destined to repeat.

> that Beloved might leave. Leave before Sethe could make
> her realize that worse than that--far worse-- ...That
> anybody white could take your whole self for anything that
> came to mind ... Dirty you so bad you forgot who you
> were and couldn't think it up. Whispering, muttering some
> justification, some bit of clarifying information to Beloved
> to explain what it had been like, and why, and how come.
> (251-2)

Sethe was willing to endure any treatment given by her child in order to secure some understanding between them. If vengeance would ease the restlessness of her child's spirit, Sethe would submit willingly. She did not want forgiveness for what she had done for it would mean there were alternatives that she had overlooked, and that was not the case. As a slave she had no right to love and protect her family, and these issues encompass what she felt most important in her understanding of freedom: "Maybe I couldn't love 'em proper in Kentucky because they wasn't mine to love. But when I got here ... there wasn't nobody in the world I couldn't love if I wanted to" (162). This right to love was rooted in what freedom meant to Sethe. Paul D understood this and expressed what freedom meant to them both: "to get to a place where you could love anything you chose--not to need permission for desire--well now, *that* was freedom"(162). To make her daughter understand that a life in slavery was comparable to no life at all was what Sethe truly sought. She also knew that neither of them could find peace until her baby's spirit understood that its life was taken out of love and a respect for life. The same understanding that Sethe wanted from her dead baby was never realized in her relationship with her sons, Howard and Buglar. Her attempt to take her sons' lives had failed, but here also there was a lack of understanding on their part as to why their mother had done this terrible thing. Their fear of her power to both give and take life made them run away. Even though Sethe wanted all her children to know the whys regarding her act of infanticide, it was Beloved's life which was sacrificed. It was her baby daughter who would never know the earthly freedom that Sethe wanted so desperately for all her children.

Morrison encourages the reader to further question the act of infanticide by juxtaposing Sethe's actions with that of natural images. This lends clarity to the repressive nature of slave existence and illuminates the need for a free and open existence. Sethe is firmly rooted in nature throughout the novel, as the scars on her back in the shape of a chokecherry tree attest. Morrison moves us from Sethe as earthbound to Sethe who is able to soar above the pull of social and legal gravity. As we see in the novel, for instance, while escaping from Sweet Home, heavy with her unborn child, Sethe at one point has to crawl. She was bound to the earth, for the condition of slavery would not release her. Once she escapes and finds refuge with Baby Suggs, however, she regains her strength and claims her freedom. We see the natural image of Sethe change with the arrival of Schoolteacher who comes to reclaim his property and negate Sethe's freedom. The description of Sethe is no longer earthbound for she has known the experience of being a free person:

> recognizing schoolteacher's hat, she heard wings. Little hummingbirds stuck their needle beaks right through her headcloth into her hair and beat their wings... Simply. She just flew. (163)

It is when Sethe is described as a bird that takes flight, unleashed from slavery, that we can clearly see Schoolteacher as the advancing predator and Sethe, along with her children, as his prey. A predator's ultimate goal is to feed from a weaker prey, and Sethe, who was not legally free, was still the weaker prey. It was only natural that she try to escape with the instincts of a trapped bird. Morrison's descriptive image emphasizes this:

> how she flew, snatching up her children like a hawk on the wing; how her face beaked, how her hands worked like claws, how she collected them every which way (157).

The reader is challenged to conceptualize Sethe's infanticide as an act of desperation rather than cold-blooded murder. These images allow us to see Sethe's behavior as a "natural" and understandable attempt to run from danger and thus an action of "natural" proportion, which, in fact, embraces sanity.

The relationship of Sethe, the childless mother, and the young woman Beloved, the motherless child, is a necessary bond that we see in the evolution of identities for both characters. We have determined that the lack of a maternal presence left Beloved undefined as a woman, but we also discover that the lack of maternal choices is what forced Sethe to the

drastic act of infanticide.[29] Morrison develops with Beloved's arrival a
maternal narrative that allows Sethe to explain her decision to commit
infanticide, releasing her from the burden of the act. By believing that
Beloved was her baby daughter, Sethe is able to reclaim past memories.

> When I put that headstone up I wanted to lay in there with
> you, put your head on my shoulder and keep you warm,
> and I would have if Buglar and Howard and Denver didn't
> need me, because my mind was homeless then. I couldn't
> lay down with you then. No matter how much I wanted to.
> I couldn't lay down nowhere in peace, back then. Now I
> can. I can sleep like the drowned have mercy. (204)

Sethe's maternal narrative frees her from the act of a repressive past
toward an opportunity to embrace herself, her family, and her community
in ways no longer made risky by slavery.

The relationship between Sethe and Beloved, the young woman,
serves as part of the process by which both women free themselves from
the pains and burdens of their past. Through their rememory we learn how
each woman's experiences converge and diverge as part of their quest for
understanding. "Someday you be walking down the road and you hear
something or see something going on. So clear. And you think it's you
thinking it up. A thought picture. But no. It's when you bump into a
rememory that belongs to somebody else"(36). Beloved for Sethe was the
reincarnation of her child, which allowed her the opportunity to bring
closure to a relationship. Sethe, for the young woman Beloved, was a
manifestation of her mother which allowed her to find answers to a
relationship that had been broken before she was able to grow from the
bond with her mother. It is the convergence of the broken relationships
between mother and daughter which brings Beloved and Sethe together.
"Sethe sees me see her..."(213) It is at the divergence of these stories, in
contrast, which occurs when Sethe leaves Beloved that she again senses
danger for her child [Beloved the baby spirit reincarnated as Beloved the
young woman]. Beloved the young woman, once left alone, goes back out
into the world, no longer needing to follow and feel secure only in the
presence of Sethe as her lost mother. Each character thus returns to the
larger community of free blacks. The experience that Sethe and Beloved
share is representative of how rememories intermingle and bump into each
other while people seek to release themselves from a repressive slave
perspective to an identity free to embrace self and community. The
connection between ancestors, family, and community as helpmates in the
identification of self makes a clear distinction between the lives of Sethe
and Beloved. It is the connection with family, and specifically a family
name, that Beloved the young woman lacked, for instance. Since Beloved
is "Disremembered and unaccounted for[she]... cannot be lost because
no one is looking for her, and even if they were, how can they call her if

they don't know her name?" (274). Baby Suggs and others who survived slavery know the importance of names all too well. Baby Suggs knew that her own name was key to making her locatable for those she cared for and not a title needed or useful in validating her legal move from slave to free. "Mrs. Baby Suggs ain't no name for a Freed Negro... Maybe not ... but Baby Suggs was all she had left of the 'husband' she claimed"(142). Without that name there was no hope of ever finding him, so:

> The two of them made a pact: whichever one got a chance to run would take it; together if possible, alone if not and no looking back ... Now how could he find or hear tell of her if she was calling herself some bill-of-sale name? (142)[30]

It is this same sense of names and connection that Sethe is made aware of by Nan, her nurse, when she was a child: "Without names, she [Sethe's mother] threw them away. You she gave the name of the black man. She put her arms around him"(62). Sethe's name is part of an oral history as well as an identification of a kinship lost but not forgotten. These connections through names are an intricate part of how ex-slaves reestablished homes, families, histories, communities, and places in the world.

In addition it is ancestral presence that provides the sense of a world in which the future matters. In the case of Beloved, she remains unguided and unaccounted for but Sethe had the ancestral presence of Baby Suggs to guide and direct her toward having a full life. Sethe was to further discover through this knowledge that claiming herself was a crucial part of freedom. Her understanding of this continued to deepen in the care of and from the teachings of Baby Suggs:

> That's how she got through the waiting for Halle. Bit by bit, at 124 and in the clearing, along with the others she had claimed herself. Freeing yourself was one thing; claiming ownership of that freed self was another.(95)

It is this lesson of claiming self that Baby Suggs preached in the clearing and that Sethe had to confront with both Beloved, the young woman as her reincarnated baby, and Paul D, a man who wanted to offer her a future. Sethe's value as a person worthy of love is what she had to realize to truly be released from the repressive sense of her life as meaningless into one a life that embraced her own value and her environment.

Baby Suggs, as an ancestral presence and the "unchurched preacher," taught many others the necessity of love and its healing force against slavery's atrocities in the clearing in the woods. When the community gathered together, it was a time of shedding and shouting away the pains that oppression had placed in slaves' lives. Baby Suggs realized what love meant in making an individual, as well as a people, whole. All who came to the clearing emptied themselves of their pain by laughing, dancing, and crying, then filled up their hearts with love. She allowed them the unconditional and unrestrained expression of self, whether it be with a twisted hip or a ravaged spirit. Grace, forgiveness, and pardon for all that they suffered was the only way to freedom. Baby Suggs told the people that "the only grace they could have was the grace they could imagine. That if they could not see it, they would not have it."(88) If they could not embrace forgiveness which aligns one to God and nature, a free perspective would be lost to them. Self forgiveness would allow them to be open to loving others as well as themselves.

The reclamation of family and the joys of love that Baby Suggs passed on to others was not overlooked on her own behalf for she spent two years looking for her eight children. She understood well the action that Sethe took for she, too, had no choice while a slave in the lives of her children. Each had been taken away from her, leaving only the memory of small faces grown unfamiliar with the passing of time. It was only through freedom bought by her son Halle, the only child she was able to keep close, that a different perspective of the world was gained. Once free, she looked for her children, but Halle's family was the only part of her kin she could locate. Because Baby Suggs was unable to unite with her children, Sethe's act of infanticide weighed heavily on her heart, but she could understand Sethe's pain. She implored God, "Beg your pardon, I beg your pardon"(152), for the helplessness of a slave mother could only be understood and explained through God's pardon. She, like the community, sought hope through God and her own sense of religion and spirituality. In asking for pardon she not only asks for forgiveness but also understanding, as this request is not just for Sethe but for herself as well. She painfully realized that freedom does not come just through loving, for the responsibility of that loving demands one *must* be prepared for the world as it comes from all directions. It demands that one shed the throes of slavery's indoctrinations and strive at all costs for a life that is "livable."

Although Baby Suggs's commitment to the power of love and healing was challenged by Sethe's act of infanticide, she was able to leave a legacy of survival through her quest for color that placed trust and choice squarely in God's nature.

It is this legacy of the quest for color and exploration of the harmless and safe things in life, in turn, that prepares Denver to face the world. Colors were the safe haven of nature that humans could embrace but never claim in Baby Suggs's view. It is in nature that one finds peace and protection, for the world of humans may ravage even the strongest person. When Denver, Baby Suggs's grandaughter, leaves the porch of #124 to ask for help, we see this perspective at work:

> The weather was warm; the day beautiful. It was April and
> everything alive was tentative. Denver wrapped her hair
> and her shoulders. In the brightest of the carnival dresses
> and wearing a stranger's shoes, she stood on the porch of
> 124 ready to be swallowed up in the world beyond the edge
> of the porch.(243)

Denver leaves a little afraid but secure in her mission, for she learned from her grandma, Baby Suggs, that the harmlessness of nature is one's only protection from the hurtfulness of humans.

Because of the experiences and histories that ancestors such as Nan and Baby Suggs acknowledged and passed on, Denver was was given a foundation for her own sense of self. With this awareness, the future appeared as a hopeful option for Denver, but even so, we can easily see how the future is not always embraced, particularly if the past is a wrenching memory. For Denver the future was not possible until she escaped the isolation of #124 created by the haunting of her dead baby sister. With the arrival of Beloved, the young woman, Denver found someone to share her life of isolation and someone to take the place of the baby ghost who had been her companion. This relationship did not last as Sethe and Beloved became obsessed with each other and the unresolved issues of their individual past. Denver was thus forced to see herself, as daughter and sister, moving away from #124. She was not released from Sethe's struggle nor was she trying to be, for she had to accept and know these experiences as a part of her own past. Before going out into the world, Denver also had to confront her own rememory as a child and daughter raised in #124. She had to accept her own fears that her mother could take her life as she had taken the life of her baby sister and acknowledge that the community had rejected her because of her mother's past. "So, it was she who had to step off the edge of the world and die because if she didn't they all would" (239). "They" meant not only the women of #124 but also the lineage that survived slavery and the atrocities of the Sweet Home plantation.

At a significant moment in the novel, Denver remembers the conversations she had with her grandma, Baby Suggs, about the past and the cost of the future.

> But you said there was no defense.
> "There ain't"
> Then what do I do?
> "Know it, and go on out the yard. Go on." (244)

"Denver knew it was on her."(243) It is the resistance in the form of female revolt and the physical and mental sacrifices for survival that Sethe, Baby Suggs, and other slave men and women made in their quest for freedom that ultimately allows Denver to step out into a world that had once shunned them all. It was the acceptance of both her ancestral and individual past through her grandmother that helped release her from the isolation of #124. This wisdom allowed Denver not to falter and to reject any need to defensively argue for any part of her family, or for herself. Denver knew that her life and that of her family would be continued only through the exercising of difficult choices, for slavery had denied Sethe and Baby Suggs any choice. Therefore, Denver represents the future of those who lived and survived in #124, for she possesses the histories, the rememories, and the ancestral teachings that provide foundation, example, and purpose in confronting a world unlike the one of her ancestors but one needful of the knowledge that her past and all pasts offer.

The disruption that we see played out in the life of Sethe further explicates the disruptive forces that resound through Denver's life and the lives of all black people in the Cincinnati community. Painful experiences of rememory are found in the lives of many. Ella, for instance, had to deal with the death of an unwanted child she bore; Stamp Paid had to cope with his inability to save his wife Vashti from being raped and exploited by their young master; Paul D had to confront the dehumanization and brutality he endured while on a chain gang while the community at large had to process and confront past whippings, rape, loss of kin, and regret over not confronting the atrocities they all knew under slavery. The community of Cincinnati struggled with reclaiming these stories of pain, shame, and sadness, which separated them not only from the family in #124 but often from each other. Their rememories meant they had to confront unnursed and unborn babies, unavenged wives and lovers, and broken minds that each had locked in the past. There was no need to defend behaviors of the past when they were trapped in the perpetual condition of misery, but there was a need to accept such experiences once survived. Paul D understood on one level his own helplessness when he was a slave and prisoner on the chain gang, but he nevertheless questions Sethe's infanticide, and he berates himself for his passive response to abuse. Sethe responds to Paul D with the same resolve that motivated her act:

> "It ain't my job to know what's worse. It's my job to know
> what is and to keep them away from what I know is terrible.
> I did that."
> "What you did was wrong, Sethe."
> "I should have gone back there? Taken my babies back
> there?"
> "There could have been a way. Some other way."
> "What way?"(165)

It is Paul D's inability to embrace rememory which keeps him from recognizing that the lack of choices Sethe confronted was just the same as it had been in his own experiences. Paul D could not tell Sethe what else she could have done, for there *was* nothing else she could have done. What he failed to recognize was that in both their stories and in all the other stories, it was not the humanity of the slave that was in question but the inhumanity of the slaveholder. In Paul D's struggle he would come to see that the slaveholder was consumed with the savagery that had been relegated to the slaves.

> In, through and after life, it spread, until it invaded the whites who had made it. Touched them every one. Changed and altered them. The screaming baboon lived under their own white skin; the red gums were their own. (198-99)

The true result of confronting rememories thus became the recognition that the possibility of finding earthly choice and control does not exist within the realm of an inhumane circumstance. For the community and Paul D, the rememories that each person bore became a matter of self-forgiveness. Only by embracing those who resisted slavery, and even those who didn't could they forgive themselves and others.

Forgiveness for the slave and ex-slave was found within the teachings of religion, which gave a sense of hope to human beings and the world. Without this hope, many saw death as the only option. The rejection of hope caused many blacks to be silent and turn away when acts of resistance were played out in the community. For the community of Cincinnati, Sethe's infanticide represented a hopelessness which caused them to respond by shunning her. The black community of Cincinnati had survived on hope and faith, which brought many through slavery to freedom. By attempting to take her children's lives, Sethe exemplified a rejection of the very things that had sustained the community. Morrison evokes the difficulties of the community in coming to terms with Sethe's actions with a passage from the Bible, Romans 9:25, placed at the beginning of the novel. In this passage, the disciple Paul speaks regarding the Gentiles and "call[s] them my people, which were not my people; and her beloved, which was not beloved." This passage sets the theme that the reader is to embrace all those who have struggled with accepting someone into their community or family of God's children. The passage also serves as a guide for understanding the relationship of Sethe to the community of Cincinnati, for the "her" that Paul speaks of in the passage is Israel. The people of Israel were loved by Paul, but they had not behaved as one who is loved, and he had to turn away from them, just as the community of Cincinnati turned away from Sethe. Romans 9:30-32 tells us that Israel was "not beloved" "Because they sought it[the law of righteousness] not by faith, but as it were by the works of the law. For they stumbled at the stumblingstone." This act of seeking a solution to problems outside one's spiritual base caused Israel to stumble. Sethe also looked for solutions outside faith and she stumbles in her act of infanticide, or so the community believed. The community supported Sethe's demanding her rights as a free woman and refuting the laws of slavery, but it could not approve her breaking the commandment of God, "Thou shalt not kill." The fact that she chose infanticide and not her faith suggests she "stumbled at the stumblingstone" and "she failed to obey her own

God-given law--which in reality was pointing to Christ."[31] Even though Sethe commits infanticide, however, the community still considers her among those who are not lost forever. Romans 9:33 goes on to say that "whosoever believeth on him [sic] shall not be ashamed." This passage suggests it is the continuing belief in God, even in mistaken choices, that allows Israel to be embraced ("Call them my people... and her beloved which was not beloved"). In a parallel fashion, the text implies, the community, is able to understand, forgive, and ultimately reclaim Sethe.

However achieved, it is the reclamation of painful experiences and the collective knowledge of slavery that move the community out of personal isolation into a united force. In considering Sethe's situation as part of a common struggle against slavery, the community decides to act. It is at the moment when the women of the community come to #124 to rescue Sethe from Beloved, whom they perceive to be evil, that Sethe confronts her darkest rememory, but also the women confront their own rememory as slave, mother, and woman. As the women approach, Sethe reflects back on the clearing where Baby Suggs preached to the community about forgiveness and acceptance through love. It was there, in the clearing, that Baby Suggs had so often preached and the community first learned of such concepts. It was there that they released much of their pain with dancing, shouting, crying, and singing and embraced themselves as worthy of both giving and receiving these things.

> For Sethe it was as though the clearing had come to her with all its heat and shimmering leaves, where the voices of women searched for the right combination, the key, the code, the sound that broke the back of words. Building voice upon voice until they found it, and when they did it was a wave of sound wide enough to sound deep water and knock the pods off chestnut trees. It broke over Sethe and she trembled like the baptized in its wash. (261)

When the moment of release came, Sethe was made new as though baptized into a new acceptance of herself and her environment. Undoubtedly, the knowledge and understanding that Baby Suggs brought to Sethe and to the community enabled them all to come together in redemptive forgiveness. By each person confronting their own rememories and thus bumping into the collective experiences of being abused and yet surviving slavery, all were enabled to gain some new sense of themselves as free--black--people.

As African Americans confront the issues of slavery, questions about healing and undoing the damage that came from that experience are at the forefront of their explorations of the past. Morrison has taken the components of survival and subjugation she has seen within the African American experience and used them as text and context for her novel. Such knowledge is also found within oral histories and myths that are alive in the African American tradition and shared experiences of survival. In an interview on *The South Bank Show* on BBC-TV in 1988, Morrison referred to the complexities of these strengths:

> On the one hand, she said, she could find historical accounts of the slave trade and slavery which gave her not only numbers but information about objects—instruments of punishment and torture, that somebody designed, like the iron bit placed under the tongue. On the other hand, there was Black oral culture, its stories and songs—of mourning, defiance and delight—but these did not tell of the appalling things recorded in the history books. Her novel attempts to inhabit that silence.[32]

Because of the many stories *not* told, myths and legacies become a resource for the exploration of the past. Morrison herself says, "That's what I mean by dusting off the myth, looking closely at it to see what it might conceal ...."[33] *Beloved* is not based on imagination and fanciful notions but on a deeper look at such legacies and a reconstruction of circumstance and situations of the past. From this a process must develop that is inclusive of a group consciousness. Marlene Nourbese Philip in "The Absence of Writing or How I Almost Became a Spy" talks about myth in just this way:

> So metaphorical life takes place, so the language becomes richer, the store of metaphor, myth and fable enlarged, and the experience transcended not by exclusion and alienation, but by inclusion in the linguistic psyche, the racial and generic memory of the group.[34]

This group memory preserves what might otherwise be lost and forgotten. Jacqueline de Weever in *Mythmaking and Metaphor in Black Women's Fiction* also studies myth and how it has been transformed to meet different cultural needs:

> Obviously a new mythology is needed to embrace all America, and this proves a very difficult undertaking. Not a new myth exactly, but a new dimension of the myth transposed into a different key. The most frequently recurring motif appearing ... is the motif of suffering that brings transformation and life ....[35]

It is this transformation of suffering that allows myth to take on a new dimension. It may well be that rememory has manifested itself in myth, for we do not pass on the story itself, but we recognize within the myth the source from which it came. Morrison's work thus becomes the compilation of legacies and myths that explore the transformation of individuals and the community. Morrison has been able to combine all these to present the reader and the critic with a work that calls upon us to rethink what we know and even "remember" those things we have forgotten we know.

Slavery and the responsibility for its existence often places contemporary audiences in a defensive position, but Morrison seeks to move to a position of moral questioning, not one of blame. She provides a framework for avoiding the fault-finding of an analyst like Barbara Hill Rigney who concludes that Morrison's characters in *Beloved* present the brutality of their lives as an indictment of the entire white race with little recognition of the aid given by abolitionists or other whites. She notes that most of Morrison's characters:

> hold the white race as a whole responsible for the historic subjugation of people of color .... The possible exception to this general indictment is Amy Denver.[36]

Even though Baby Suggs condemns white people in her dying words, however, it is clear this is not Morrison's goal. She does not offer only white characters such as Schoolteacher as strictly abusers of power but balances them with those whites who use power in more humane efforts such as abolition. But in my view such a discussion is irrelevant to the novel. I agree with Linda Krumholz, who in her article "The Ghosts of Slavery: History and Recovery in Toni Morrison's *Beloved*," sees characters such as Baby Suggs as transcending the categories Rigney imposes:

> [they] represent an epistemological and discursive philosophy...in which morality is not preset in black and white categories of good and evil; "good" or "evil" spring from the *methods* of categorizing and judging, of understanding and distributing knowledge.[37]

Krumholz goes on to note that race is not an inherently divisive issue but instead, in the context of slavery and oppression, was based on domination and an abuse of power that invoked race to maintain that domination. Echoing this perspective, Sandi Russell, in *Render Me My Song*, describes *Beloved* as "far from the usual slave depictions: bad whites, good blacks. Each person carries his or her own complexity,"[38] while Judith Thurman, in her review of *Beloved* in *The New Yorker*, says:

> it is not primarily a historical novel, and Morrison does not attempt ... to argue the immorality of slavery on rational grounds .... As the reader struggles with its fragments and mysteries, he keeps being startled by flashes of his own reflection in them.[39]

Although responsibility is assignable to any act, the novel is mostly concerned with how one survives such acts and moves beyond them to a healthier existence.

Beloved is not a story to pass on, but one that causes you to "Know it, and go on out the yard. Go on"(244). Reading it, we learn that one is not necessarily imprisoned by cruel acts for they can be seen as acts of freedom and love committed against madness and a living death. It is not wise to silence the story by closing the entrance to #124, and you must not try and close yourself off from the pain of "Sixty million or more." Ancestral experience shared transcends the printed word and allows one to see an issue as it is expressed within the circumstance of a people. *Beloved* urges one to look into the depths of relationships and how they influence the individual and, in turn, the community. There are many stories like Sethe's, Paul D's, Ella's, Jeny's, Stamp Paid's, Baby Suggs's, Beloved's, Halle's, and Denver's, and in knowing them, we may decipher the code they lived and died by. The identification of the past which serves to express and explore the parameters of choice or the lack of it pays homage to the potential and power that lies within the oppressed and opens the door to love that can heal or bring hope to the lost, damaged, and repressed. It is through this process of embracing the past in all its pain and glory that identities evolve to form a healthy people.

The stories have not ended, for there are those yet in the world who are beloved and bewildered. However their rememory is revealed to the collective perception, it is the lesson of survival that moves a people forward. Even though the language of Sethe's mother may be forgotten and the haunting voices that came from and surrounded #124 be silenced, we still understand the message. Just as Stamp Paid noticed "something was wrong with the order of the words" (172) as he listened at the door of #124 and Sethe remembered "different words" (62) which described her mother's language, we still get from the past what we need to know: "the message—that was, and had been there, all along" (62).

We can conclude from our exploration of the novel *Beloved* that even though slavery had a crippling and silencing effect on the perspective of the slave and ex-slave, a determination arose to embrace the value of oneself and family, and people went to extraordinary lengths to maintain their human rights even unto death. Through confrontation with one's environment and one's self the slave perspective is stripped away and the free perspective emerges. Through these lessons of survival for the African American, identity and the possibilities of choice in the business of life come into view. In *Beloved* as in the other texts examined here, it is the oral and personal histories as they capture ancestral knowledge and community mythology that define the themes of positive change in slave narratives, biographies, autobiographies, and fiction by African American artists.

Notes

1. "During slavery, white mental health workers pointed to the high incidence of mental illness among blacks in the North--there was ten times more mental illness in the North than in the South--and concluded that slavery was a benign institution which protected inferior blacks from the stresses of a competitive society. Traditionally, any black who asserted himself was labelled a 'crazy' or 'uppity nigger' who ought to be incarcerated in a mental hospital or a prison." Alvin Poussaint, *Why Blacks Kill Blacks* (New York: Emerson Hall, 1972), 50.

2. Lerone Bennett, Jr., *Before the Mayflower: A History of Black America*, 5th ed. (New York: Penguin Books, 1984) 87. And see Don E. Fehrenbacher, *Slavery, Law, and Politics: The Dred Scott Case in Historical Perspective* (New York: Oxford University Press, 1981), 7-8.

3. Lawrence N. Houston, "Frustration and Adjustment," *Psychological Principles and the Black Experience* (New York: University Press of America, 1990), 111.

4. Roberta Rubenstein, "Pariahs and Community," Henry Louis Gates, Jr. and K.A. Appiah, eds., *Toni Morrison: Critical Perspectives Past and Present* (New York: Amistad Press, 1993), 126-155. Rubenstein further says of community that "The figure of the pariah is clearly central to Morrison's vision, as the emblem of different levels and forms of exclusion. In her fiction the community is understood as both a specific structure--and the vehicle through which behavior is expressed and reinforced" (154). Morrison herself states of community that the civilization of black people that lives apart from but in juxtaposition to other civilizations is a pariah relationship. See Claudia Tate, *Black Women Writers at Work* (New York: Continuum, 1983), 126,129.

5. Infanticide as a part of the slave woman's experiences has been considered a form of abortion in many cases because of its link to known West African traditions. In these traditions, a child was not considered human until nine days after birth. If the child died prior to the nine days, it was thought to become a wandering spirit. Barbara Bush brings clarity to this issue when she stated that infanticide, among other means of slave women's control of their bodies, "does not demand a detailed debate with quantitative historians but a closer examination of the complex relationship between cultural resistance and material conditions as they affect slave women's attitudes to childbirth." Barbara Bush, *Slave Women in Caribbean Society 1650-1830* (Bloomington: Indiana University Press, 1990), 121, 148. This tradition, along with poor nutrition and the weariness of slave mothers offered a rationale for high infant mortality rates and child mortality rates, which meant that fewer than two out of three black children lived past the age of ten between 1850 and 1860. Jacqueline Jones, *Labor of Love, Labor of Sorrow: Black Women,Work*

and the Family, from Slavery to the Present, (New York: Vintage Books, 1995), 35. Even though there are cases of infanticide similar to Margaret Garner's, the official response has been that these were exceptions. The fact that slave mothers recognized these acts as murder encouraged slaveholders and teachers of Christian doctrine to evoke religion as the rationale for assurance of infanticide as "special circumstances" rather than a defiant statement to God and man. Eugene Genovese, *Roll, Jordan, Roll: The World the Slaves Made* (New York: Vintage Books, 1976), 497.

6. Genovese, *Roll, Jordan, Roll,* 597 and 598.

7. Angela Davis, "Reflections on the Black Woman's Role in the Community of Slaves," *Black Scholar,* Vol. 3, No. 4 (December 1971), 3-15.

8. Toni Morrison, "Rediscovering Black History" *New York Times Magazine,* 11 August 1974, 13-21.

9. Gloria Naylor and Toni Morrison, "A Conversation," *The Southern Review,* Vol. 21, No. 3 (Summer 1985), 567-593.

10. Stanley Feldstein, *Once a Slave: The Slave's View of Slavery* (New York: William Morrow, 1970), 90.

11. Middleton Harris, Morris Levitt, Roger Furman, and Ernest Smith, eds. *The Black Book* (New York: Random House, 1974), 10-11.

12. Harris et al., *Black Book,* 10.

13. Madness has carried many meanings over the ages, but in all cases it addresses a person's confrontation with truth and lies, life and death. Michel Foucault states that "Madness is the purest, most total form of *quid pro quo*; it takes the false for the true, death for life, man for woman. . . . But it is also the most rigorously necessary form of the *quid pro quo* in the dramatic economy, for it needs no external element to reach a true resolution." *Madness and Civilization: A History of Insanity in the Age of Reason* (New York: Pantheon Books, 1965), 33. Using Foucault's model, we can say that those whites who saw Margaret Garner as mad separated her actions from truth when in fact she was able to discover truth away from the "external element" that slavery represented. Garner was able to see that slavery created a reality that in fact was a lie. It was false that blacks were not human, and it was false that death could not release one from bondage to freedom.

14. A few months after *Beloved* was published, Morrison did an interview with *City Limits Magazine* in March of 1988. The interview, "Living Memories," is where she discusses memory as a primary issue in her novel.

15. American Social History Project under the Direction of Herbert G. Gutman, *Who Built America?: Working People and The Nation's*

Economy, Politics, Culture and Society (New York: Pantheon Books, 1989), 287-89.

16. This incident was recorded by a physician in a Nashville, Tennessee, medical journal from 1849. See Herbert G. Gutman, *The Black Family in Slavery and Freedom 1750-1925* (New York: Pantheon Books, 1976), 80-82.

17. Gary B. Nash, *Red, White, and Black: The Peoples of Early North America* (Englewood Cliffs, NJ: Prentice Hall Publications, 1992), 196.

18. Nash, *Red, White, and Black,* 171.

19. W.E.B. DuBois stated, "But one thing I shall never forgive, neither in this world nor the world to come: Its [white South] wanton and continued and persistent insulting of the black womanhood which it sought and seeks to prostitute to its lust," W.E.B. DuBois, *Darkwater: Voices from Within the Veil* (New York: Schocken Books, 1969), 172. The corruption of home which confronted so many black men continued to reverberate in the black male consciousness well into the twentieth century.

20. The use of and contempt for the female slave was tempered only by the motives and perspective of the master and had little to do with her physical condition. See Angela Davis, "Reflections on the Black Woman's Role in the Community of Slaves," *Black Scholar*, Vol. 3, No. 4 (December 1971), 3-15.

21. Nash, *Red, White, and Black,* 196.

22. Paul D. Escott and David R. Goldfield, eds., *Major Problems in the History of the American South, Volume I: The Old South* (Lexington, MA: D.C. Heath Publications, 1990), 582-90.

23. When speaking of the efforts of others, reference is being made to blacks who escaped and might return; blacks who escaped and aided in the cause for all to be free; blacks who hoped that others might allow their children a free life or if held in bondage, a master whose heart had not been hardened.

24. Jacqueline Jones, *Labor of Love, Labor of Sorrow*, 58.

25. Toni Morrison, *Beloved* (New York: Penguin Books, 1988). Page numbers in parentheses in this chapter refer to this edition of the novel.

26. Toni Morrison, "Rootedness: The Ancestor as Foundation," *Black Women Writers (1950-1980): A Critical Evaluation*, ed. Mari Evans (New York: Doubleday, 1984), 343.

27. Henry Louis Gates, Jr., *Figures in Black: Words, Signs, and the "Racial" Self* (New York: Oxford University Press, 1987), 101. Gates discusses the danger that existed when a slave was confined to his or her ability to recall the only base of his or her existence:

> For the dependence upon memory made the slave, first and
> foremost, a slave to himself or herself, a prisoner of his or
> her own power or recall. Within such a time machine, as
> it were, not only had the slave no fixed reference points,
> but also his or her own past could exist only as members
> without support, as text without footnots, as the clock
> without two hands. With such a tyrannical concept of time,
> the slave has no past beyond memory; the slave lived at no
> time past the point of recollection. (101)

28. One of the key concerns for many readers is whether or not
Beloved is a ghost of Sethe's baby or whether she is a whole person in her
own troubled space. I think Morrison intentionally plays to both concepts.
One belief of some African cultures that deterred infanticide was "that the
dead, of whatever age, take revenge on the living." (Bush, *Slave Women*,
148) If a child died within the nine days before its humanity was realized,
it was considered a harmless spirit but still a spirit. We are left in either
case with a wandering spirit as a result of the act of infanticide. Whether
Beloved is perceived of as a spirit or a person in her own troubled space,
her struggle for the reclamation of her past as a means to her own
identification is exemplary of the African American struggle, and the
suffering that she experienced is reflective of the plight of some sixty
million or more Africans who sailed the Middle Passage but never crossed
it.

29. Marianne Hirsh, in "Maternal Narratives: Cruel Enough to Stop
the Blood," talks about the maternal perspective in her discussion of
Beloved. She says of Sethe:

> It [her maternal narrative] allows her both to recognize her
> love for Beloved and her love for herself. With this novel,
> Toni Morrison has ... opened the space for maternal
> narrative in feminist fiction.

This essay addresses the "great unwritten story" regarding
motherhood as explored by Adrienne Rich in 1976. Hirsh's essay is found
in Henry Louis Gates, Jr. and K.A. Appiah, eds., *Toni Morrison: Critical
Perspectives Past and Present* (New York: Amistad, 1993), 272-283.
Also see Hortense Spillers' "A Hateful Passion, A Lost Love" in the same
volume, which discusses women's relations in the novel *Sula*.

30. It is important to note that the "bill of sale" name and the names
slaves used among themselves were not always the same.

31. *The New International Version Study Bible*, Kenneth Bacher, et
al., ed. (Grand Rapids, MI: Zondervan, 1985), 1720.

32. The interview with Toni Morrison is summarized by Gina Wisker,
ed., *Black Women's Writing* (New York: St. Martin's Pess, 1993), 121.

33. Thomas Leclair, "The Language Must Not Sweat: A Conversation with Toni Morrison," *Toni Morrison: Critical Perspectives Past and Present*, 369-77.

34. Marlene Nourbese Philip, "The Absence of Writing or How I Almost Became a Spy," *She Tries Her Tongue, Her Silence Softly Breaks* (East Haven, CT: Inbooks, 1995), 10-25.

35. Jacqueline de Weever, *Mythmaking and Metaphor in Black Women's Fiction* (New York: St. Martin's Press, 1991), 13-14.

36. Barbara Hill Rigney, "The Disremembered and Unaccounted For," *Toni Morrison: Critical Perspectives Past and Present*, Henry Louis Gates, Jr. and K.A. Appaih, (New York: Amistad, 1993), 62-73.

37. Linda Krumholz, "The Ghost of Slavery: History and Recovery in Toni Morrison's *Beloved*," *African American Review*, Vol. 26, No. 3 (1992), 395-408.

38. Sandi Russell, *Render Me My Song: African-American Women Writers from Slavery to the Present* (New York: St. Martin's Press, 1990), 180.

39. Judith Thurman, "A House Divided," *The New Yorker* (2 November 1987), 175.

CHAPTER 4

Alice Walker's *The Color Purple*

Racism, Sexism, and Kinship
in the Process of Self-Actualization

T*he Color Purple* has a special place within the process of historical reclamation for it discusses continuing attitudes of resistance to the dominant culture's political and social agendas while revealing silences within the community that have been unavailable to historical renderings of any kind. Particularly during the period of segregation, agendas by white America intruded on black communities, threatening their lives and placing limits on their individual and collective potentials. Walker shows through the interconnectedness of the public and the private as well as the local and the intercontinental, the dynamics of intrusion into people's lives and the forces that exist for resistance and change. As we explore intrusions into the black community, we can also see that an individual's move toward self-actualization is the struggle between public and private definitions of self that have been distorted by racist and sexist notions of human potential and value. We understand as well that kinship and community are necessary components by which one unravels lies, secrets, and information about the past while giving voice to the pain that one may have endured. It is from these relationships, according to Walker, and the degendering of the forces of the universe that the individual and the community discover or reclaim any concept of "I."

In *The Color Purple*, Celie, the main character, struggles to emerge as a woman within an environment that rejects her ancestral legacies, while misrepresenting and denigrating her place as child, daughter, lover, woman, mother, and wife. She is initially deprived of knowledge about her family history, a strong and sustained link to family through the exchange of letters with her sister, and the experience of nurturing and loving her own children. Without these family ties, Celie remains isolated and undefined beyond the stereotypes given her roles. It is through the restored influences of friendship, kinship, and community, on the other hand, that awareness and knowledge of history and the world offer liberation for Celie. It is also such influences that may produce a reconnection with and discovery of identity for any who have been separated from family and ancestral knowledge.

It is to emphasize Celie's disenfranchisement that Walker locates *The Color Purple* in the early twentieth century, a time of legal segregation as well as economic and political limitations for blacks. This was partly a result of a post-Civil War America, which conferred citizenship to blacks but left most economic and political opportunities basically unrealized. Because of this, many blacks continued to live in close proximity to the same areas they inhabited before the Civil War since there were few alternatives.[1] The South's dominant class of whites, whose economic and social difficulties were a result of the war, sought its own self-sufficiency rather than attending to any aspirations of blacks.[2] The major focus thus became maintenance of white political and economic power at all costs and recapture of whatever gains were lost during the period of Reconstruction. One of the results was that blacks were totally disenfranchised.[3] While the right of citizenship had been gained and then lost by blacks, their treatment had changed very little. They were still considered a racially inferior group, existing for the exploitation of the dominant white culture. To perpetuate this control and thus maintain easy availability of labor, the South operated with distinctly separate communities of blacks and whites. This legal and economic structuring of communities barred blacks from access to power while subjecting them to the whims of the dominant white culture. Regional acceptance of the segregation of races and the disenfranchisement of blacks was reflective of overall national sentiment as expressed through rulings in court cases such as *Plessy v. Ferguson* (1896), *Williams v. Mississippi* (1898), *Giles v. Harris* (1903) and *Giles v. Teasley* (1904).[4] (The major court case legalizing segregation was *Plessy v. Ferguson* in 1896, which legitimized laws segregating schools, neighborhoods, parks, railroad cars, restrooms, and any public facilities.)[5] With both legal and physical separation in place, interaction between the two communities occurred only from specific intentions or intrusion of whites into black affairs.

With blacks as a powerless presence in the South, their behavior could be responded to in ways that intruded upon their legal but unenforced rights. Since there was no real penalty to pay by whites for the treatment of blacks, such intrusions were a common occurrence in the lives and communities of black Americans. These intrusions ranged from entering one's home without knocking to rape and murder. The most severe intrusions into the black community were lynchings. Lynchings, retribution for whatever the white community thought merited mob actions, became commonplace occurrences in the South at the turn of the century.[6] It is, in fact, the lynching of Celie's father, based on a real incident in Memphis in 1892, which clearly roots the characters within the social and political conditions of the time and serves to establish the powerlessness of the community to protect itself.[7] Celie's father was a farmer and ran a store in the local black community that threatened the economic control of the white community. Because of his financial success with his store and his farm, whites sought to eliminate him as competition in securing the black community's dollars. As portrayed by Walker fictionally, economic gains were seen as a threat in historical reality, too, for they would allow blacks greater opportunities to move in arenas outside of their segregated communities. It is this threat, represented by Celie's father, that caused the white community to murder him. We do not know if Celie's father-in-law was besieged with threats or was even a victim of brutality, but he does sell off much of his land over the years as a defense against this possible physical danger.

Individuals who rejected the intrusions of the white community and were not victims of outright lynchings were nonetheless subjected to retaliation that could not be deterred by legal or moral means. Sofia, initially the most powerful woman in the story, resists the most powerful members in the white community, the mayor and his wife. Although it is the mayor's wife who asks Sofia to work for her and is the one openly refused, it is her husband, wielding his political power and his fist, who defeats Sofia. This intrusion into Sofia's life, which results in her imprisonment for over eleven and a half years, constitutes a long sentence for "sassing the mayor's wife(89)." Her punishment, continued after prison by being forced to work for the mayor's wife and their daughter's family, attests to the limitless nature of these intrusions. The unannounced visits to Sofia's house by Eleanor Jane, the mayor's daughter, represents the potential for interminable political subjugation in that Eleanor Jane's male child, Sofia's charge, is destined to become like his father and grandfather who assume their own superiority to her. Sofia had rejected this family in her youth and, in her determination to overcome their demands, was beaten down. She was made to realize that legal, political, and economic oppression carried a much greater force than her own personal strength or that of the community. Even if aided by a strong black man, Sofia could not be saved, for political dominance and the legal rejection of her rights were stronger than her personal fearlessness.

Within this segregated environment and the rural existence common among black communities, isolation often bred a silence about one's victimization that was designed to forestall further interference into one's life. However, this silence was a double-edged sword, according to Walker, for it allowed destructive behaviors within family units to go unchecked and unchallenged. We see these internally damaging forces at work when Celie suffers repeated physical abuse and sexual assault. Her stepfather's moral laxity and his disrespect for women are examples of what Walker will interrogate in the novel as internalized racism in the community being directed at women whose abuse is met with the same silence adopted for protection against white abuse. This attitude toward women, and Celie in particular, allowed her stepfather to intrude upon every aspect of her life just as white society had intruded, unchecked, into the lives of the black community. Furthermore, the failure of the community to confront such behaviors within the family undercuts its potential to band together to confront the abuse everyone suffered from whites.

The destructive attitude of the black community toward silence regarding assaultive family behaviors on the one hand and its collective efforts to protect its members from whites on the other reflect the contradictory forces within the community in the wake of slavery. Michele Wallace, in her essay "Blues for Mr. Spielberg," comments on this ambiguity and its destructive effect on the individual:

> On the one hand, the community may offer certain protection and compensations. On the other, the community is a result of segregation and poverty, not fraternal feelings or collective purpose. And so the protagonist, usually radically individualistic, either endures some degree of spiritual alienation from the community as the price of creative identity or is destroyed/consumed. Even when deliverance comes, it is apt to be in the form of exile, hibernation, catastrophe, madness or death.[8]

Wallace identifies a key complexity of black life during this period since freedom had to be redefined after slavery in adaptation to a world that barred ex-slaves from true citizenship even though they were emancipated. The ability to move forward often meant individuals had to leave the isolated community and return as part of the force that would aid in its progress. We see this cycle of departure and return played out in the novel not only in the America where Celie resides but also in Africa. Here, the dispossessed Africans acculturated in America return to the motherland seeking a place with their new found knowledge and sense of themselves. One of Walker's most incisive points, in fact, is how intrusions endured by the black community in America are similar to those the African community of the Olinkas were forced to suffer from the European colonizers.[9] Each community has no choice but to submit to the whims and mandates of the dominant group. We discover the prime example of this in Nettie's letters, which describe how the Olinka people's home and way of life were threatened and eventually destroyed by plans for a new road and a rubber plant.

The complexities of these relations between colonizer and oppressed are demonstrated in the novel by the duality of Corrine and Samuel's missionary work. On the one hand, it is another form of Western intrusion as it tries to affect lives and communities that are different in many ways from the lives of the missionaries. Even African American missionaries are imbued with a kind of paternalism to the Africans they attempt to convert. On the other hand, Samuel, Corrine, and Nettie were aware of an ambivalence and even indifference towards them and the work they did, while there was a sense of their own destinies being tied to the lives of all black people. Missionary work for the African Americans, unlike the straightforward colonizing efforts of white Europeans, grew out of kinship ties and a sense of community with Africans and sought to mitigate the destructiveness of white intrusion into the lives of black people on both sides of the Atlantic. For the African American missionary, the sharing of pasts and destinies often moved the colonizer-exploited relationship to one of greater knowledge and reclaimed kinship that had previously been hidden, devalued, or ignored.

The lengthy description of Corrine and Samuel's missionary work in Africa appears to be a break from the novel's initial themes of identity and empowerment. In actuality, it extends these issues to the diaspora, encompassing all black communities. Walker gives us Nettie's experiences in Africa as part of the expanded sense of one's place in the world. Nettie's letters, in turn, equip Celie to embrace and strengthen her own identity, protected from an intrusive force that isolates and restricts her potential for being black and a woman. It is this knowledge about the world outside of Georgia that opens possibilities to a future for Celie. Her realization of an African family beyond the boundaries of America's colonial plan expands Celie's notion of personal struggle to one of common battle with a superior force wielded by the white world over black people as a group.

Recognizing her kinship with Africans is the first step in Celie's journey toward a collective, empowering identity that transcends personal isolation, while the second is her dawning awareness that gender division in Africa is not unlike that which she sees around her. Nettie describes the sexist perspective of the Olinka tribe in ways that open Celie's eyes to the assumptions governing her own abusive treatment. In one such letter, for instance, Nettie describes what she has been told an Olinka woman's role is:

> A girl is nothing to herself; only to her husband can she become something. What can she become? I asked. Why, she said, the mother of his children. (162)

One's value as a woman, in other words, was largely based on the usefulness of her reproductive function.[10] To be without reproductive capacity relegated a barren wife like Celie to the role of a drudge. Celie's ability to bear children was destroyed because of the lust of her stepfather who negated her womanhood except for his own purposes. As a result, Pa represents Celie to Mr.-- only in terms of her ability to work:

> She ugly. He say. But she ain't no stranger to hard work....
> And God done fixed her. You can do everything just like
> you want to and she ain't gonna make you feed it or clothe
> it. She ain't smart either .... But she can work like a man.
> (9)

Her worth is discussed as though she were the "mule of the world," in Zora Neale Hurston's terms.[11] Nettie, on the other hand, was considered valuable because she was "fresh." She had not been spoiled by incest and childbirth, but even so, Nettie's value was still ultimately based on whatever role of usefulness society had deemed for her, such as being a schoolteacher. This common bond of worth being based on utility, exclusive of individuality and personal identity, created a sad but revealing kinship between black women of Africa and America. It is in part the constructed roles of gender, Walker suggests, that have intruded into the lives of black women of the diaspora and have led to their subjugation and isolation. It is also the commonality of these constructs that bind women in their oppression throughout the diaspora and opens for Celie, paradoxically, the way out.

Having established the poles of racism and sexism as fault lines splitting the black community in Africa and the American South, the novel explores the complex dynamic between them, one that is played out largely on the bodies of black women. Barbara Christian in *Black Feminist Criticism* provides a useful perspective on this interplay when she says:

> The comparison-contrast between male-female
> relationships in Africa and the black South suggest that
> sexism for black women in America does not derive from
> racism, though it is qualitatively affected by it(94).[12]

Christian's insight about the interconnectedness of race and gender oppression is valuable for exploring one of the novel's major subjects, the sexual objectification of nonwhite women by white and black men alike. The tendency of the community to equate women's worth with their biological roles in reproduction is extended into further sexual objectification by its internalization of racist beauty standards in America. Both standards for measuring female worth stem largely from slavery itself when slave women were valued as (re)producers of field labor and white skin was associated with power and privilege. Horrace Mann Bond, among others, refers to the importance of skin color among blacks themselves as a result of this system when he describes the material advantages of some lighter-shaded ex-slaves who went on to form an elite group:

> [Favored slaves were] slaves who were frequently related
> to their white masters by kinship and by occupation, and
> thus more likely than negro field hands to receive material
> assistance in obtaining both a sound economic base and an

education from their master and their ex-masters after the
Civil War.[13]

Even though light skin was often, but not always, the result of rape and
sexual exploitation, a mixed blood heritage was seen by the dominant
culture as having a positive effect on the abilities and appearance of blacks
and thus afforded them more status.[14] In privileging light skin tone, whites
fostered a continuation of controls over the black community and a class
system based on racialized opportunity.

> Throughout the slave period and on into the 20th century,
> Whites manipulated the color tensions in Black America
> as a means of control and subordination. Fair-skinned
> Blacks, for example, were given special privileges and
> urged to look down on darker Blacks. At the same time,
> dark-skinned Blacks were taught by whips and chains to
> despise themselves and their features. After Emancipation,
> Whites favored certain fair-skinned Blacks by making sure
> they got an education and by recommending them for
> whatever jobs were available to the Black community.[15]

The result was that these preferences toward lighter-skinned blacks left a
destructive legacy well into the twentieth century and perpetuated lines of
division among people of the black community. Skin tone served as a
visual guide to whether one was noticed, loved, accepted, or even thought
worthy of life. This racial construct intruded deeply into physical and
emotional self-images.

Walker suggests that this divisive legacy of slavery is intensified by
gender constructs inherited from partiarchial parts of Africa as well as the
American South. This perspective stands as a legacy from writers such as
Anna Julia Cooper and Ida B. Wells. Hazel Carby in "In the Quiet,
Undisputed Dignity of My Womanhood" talks about the uses of race and
gender as oppressive tools and how Ida B. Wells addressed those issues
head on:

> [Wells] was, to put it bluntly, an "uppity" black woman
> with an analysis of the relationship among political
> terrorism, economic oppression, and conventional codes
> of sexuality and morality that has still to be surpassed in
> its incisive condemnation of the patriarchal manipulation
> of race and gender.[16]

Codes of repressive sexuality and morality in combination with the
internalized racial component of skin tone only served to complicate an
already difficult series of barriers and misconceptions about human value
that pervaded the black and white communities as a result of slavery's
manipulative tools of repression and control.

Skin tone for the African Americans as an internalized barometer of
self-worth permeated the social and political realm of the community well

past its inception during slavery and became a part of the social and literary development of black communities thereafter. Individuals of lighter skin tones, mulattoes, were provided with greater opportunities in society because the mixing of blood assumed an improved genealogy and thus a greater propensity toward assimilation into the majority white society.[17] By the turn of the century, after Emancipation, the mulatto elite emerged as the most educated and politically active group in the black community. Because this historical ascendance is referenced in Walker's choice of a very dark heroine, it is important to review briefly the impact of mulatto politics on writers at the turn of the century. W.E.B. Du Bois, a major figure in the black community, sought rights for the community based on the light-skinned privilege of relatively well-positioned mulattos:

> An essay by W. E. B. Du Bois called on the Negro community to "produce a College-educated class whose mission would be to serve and guide the progress of the masses." Among those Du Bois designated to help lead the way were twenty-one men and two women, all but one of whom were mulatto. This list of leaders, [was] popularly known as the "Talented Tenth" (a reference to the "Top" 10 percent of the Negro population).[18]

Although blacks of darker complexion were educated and rose to positions of power, and other mulattoes, such as Booker T. Washington, disagreed with the notion that the talented tenth could effectively aid the average black, the issue of skin tone created a dramatic division in the black community. Marcus Garvey, in questioning the mulatto elite, for instance, considered that "unadulterated Blackness was equivalent to spotless morality, a position that outraged members of the mulatto elite."[19] These racialized differences were thus internalized deeply by both the black and white communities.

Many writers of the late nineteenth century such as Frances Ellen Watkins Harper and Charles Chesnutt reflected these ideas by featuring tragic mulatto characters as protagonists.[20] The logic behind this narrative strategy was that such characters would be the most likely to appeal to the powerful white reading public and to encode the humanity of the character and the black race in general. These characters, who primarily were committed to uplifting their race, also served as moral guides interrogating Jim Crow segregation by their own victimization as people with high character, intelligence, and worth. In addition to their illegitimate exclusion from roles and lifestyles reserved for whites, mulatto characters suffered from anomie, a sense that they belonged nowhere in a world divided by the concept of black and white skin color, black and white communities. The drama of a mulatto protagonist created opportunities to problematize such polarities while reinforced by the fact that most writers were themselves mulatto. The privileging of light skin within the black community, of course, reflected the racialized opportunity for success that operated in the nation at large, but the consequences were far reaching and often destructive.

The trope of the tragic mulatto continued well into the twentieth century as writers of the Harlem Renaissance continued to struggle with the restrictions of segregation. It is a major theme of literary landmarks such as Nella Larsen's *Quicksand* (1928) and *Passing* (1929), Jessie Fauset's *Plum Bun* (1928) and *There Is Confusion* (1924), and James Weldon Johnson's, *The Autobiography of an Ex-Colored Man* (1912). Unlike the earlier period, however, and this would be a development to which Alice Walker returns, discrimination within the black community itself began to be addressed in this literature. Although the tendency was still to marginalize characters of darker complexion, the complexity of the African American experience began to be addressed through dark protagonists as we see in George Schuyler's *Black No More* (1931) and Wallace Thurman's *The Blacker the Berry*(1929).

Schuyler, Thurman, and others "satirized the subject of race and color and dared to poke fun at a Black woman who was miserably unhappy because of her skin color."[21]

Contemporary writers have extended such investigations considerably. For instance Gwendolyn Brooks's autobiographical novella *Maude Martha* (1953) conflates the writer herself with a dark-skinned protagonist, and Toni Morrison's *The Bluest Eye* (1970) presents tragedies are fueled by internalized racist concepts in the character of a very dark child who is treated cruelly for being black in a white supremacist culture. Alice Walker participates in contemporary revision of the tragic mulatto trope by featuring a dark woman at the center of her fictional concerns and by describing her female characters in ways that encode the historical racial hierarchy of outward appearance and superficial judgment. It is in fact the women of Walker's community who are the major recipients of the idea that skin tone is a visual barometer of worth. Metaphors comparing women to inanimate and unimportant objects, for instance, abound while women's skin color is foregrounded as a standard of validation:

> Shug Avery black as my shoe. (21)
> [Annie Julia was] Not so pretty, say Carrie,...Just that head of hair. She too Black.(21)
> Pretty, [Harpo] tell me [about Sofia]. Bright. [You mean] Smart? Naw, Bright skin. (31)
> Say, do you really love me, [says Squeak] or just my color? (102)
> You black, you pore, you ugly, you a woman. [Say Mr--] Goddam, you nothing at all.(213)
> What would she [Shug] love? [asks Celie] My hair is short and kinky...My skin dark. My nose just a nose. My lips

just lips. My body just any woman's body going through
the changes of age. Nothing special here for nobody to
love. (266)

All of these indicators of worth give little if any value to the individual
who actually, even if unconsciously, resides in a much broader space in
the universe than the limits of artificial cultural standards. The
inappropriate emphasis placed on skin color is compounded by its
significance in determining occupational status as well. Just as Celie was
slated for a life of exploitation and drudgery because she was dark-skinned
with "nappy hair," for instance, Nettie was slotted to become a school
teacher because of her lighter skin and long hair. The relegation of
privilege on the basis of approximation to whiteness was so completely
embraced that even Celie invested her hopes in Nettie, while accepting
her own limited role: "It nearly kill me to think she might marry somebody
like Mr.-- or wind up in some white lady kitchen" (17). Celie did not fear
such a fate for herself for she had been continually told of her lack of value,
"Nobody love me" (117) Thus, her true person and potential were "not
noticed," and what beauty she had was "walked by."
     We can see that Celie is damaged by constructed roles based on race
and gender division and that she is at first a compilation of others'
descriptions and values. As long as she remains within these constructs,
she is helpless before her subjugation. She knows women who fare better
than she, but she cannot include herself among those worthy of such
treatment. Celie willing takes Nettie's place with Mr--, for example,
because she sees little value in her own person. Since her role as wife and
caretaker of Mr's-- children was the place she was given as a person of
low worth, she feels she deserves few if any options. It is her position as
a site of racialized and sexualized dominance codes that does not allow
Celie to fight for a more equitable role in life. She knows only that a very
dark woman who has no children of her own to raise and no ability to
produce more, no mother or aunt to protect her, and no "beauty" to entice
men cannot expect a better fate.

     Having defined the major points of Celie's subjugation, which she
gradually comes to question as she learns about social construction of race
and gender issues in Africa, Walker sets out to deconstruct the isolation
on which they rest. Nettie's letters are key to this process, of course, as is
Shug's arrival, but women's work becomes an incisive trajectory toward
self-love as well. Work is shown as a way to build trust among women
and to learn from multiple perspectives while fostering the continuation
of the community.[22] It is through work relationships that women in
particular get to know and care about each other while discovering new
things about themselves and their world. The making of quilts,
specifically, acts as a metaphor of women's ability to create whole and
useful products or selves, as it were, as the result of their interaction. Such
collective, creative, and useful activity brings broader experiences into
women's lives, while challenging the roles designated to them by society.

Quilting was not only a matter of domestic need, but it was also the beginning point of Celie's personal development. She begins a quilt, for example, after she realizes her advice to Harpo to beat Sofia was due to her own restricted existence. "I say it cause you do what I can't... Fight (42)." Those who help Celie in making this quilt expand her understanding of that restriction and thus help her to change it. The quilt pattern they select is aptly called "Sister's Choice." Using the possessive form of sister makes personal and individual what each woman brings to the collective whole. Sofia, Shug, and Celie come together at different intervals to work on the quilt with each bringing different levels of experience toward the production of this useful article which is simultaneously Celie's blossoming autonomy.

> How you sew this damn thing ? she (Shug) say... Me [Celie] and Sofia work on the quilt. Got it frame up on the porch. Shug Avery donate her old yellow dress for scrap....(61)

The bits of cloth each woman brings, symbolic of the lives they bring to Celie, are pieces of things once individually owned that are transformed into something new, beautiful, useful, and collectively constructed. Such gatherings for female work and sharing occur throughout the novel to varying degrees when Shug mentors Mary Agnes as a singer or Sofia cares for Mary Agnes's daughter so that she can apprentice in St.Louis. Such supportive relationships help each woman to secure a greater awareness of her individuality, identity, and growth. It is also through such experiences of sharing that each comes to contemplate the world and where she might fit. Seated between Shug and Albert while quilting, Celie comments:

> For the first time I think about the world. What the world got to do with anything, I think. Then I see myself sitting there quilting tween Shug Avery and Mr.--- ...For the first in my life, I feel just right(60).

From this integrated and collective understanding of her work connections, Celie can profoundly explore her place in the household, community, and the world.

The close and productive relationships that women are able to establish in the novel despite extenuating circumstances that might make them adversaries are shown as threatening to the male characters who resist transforming their own lives as well. In this way Walker explores the very real tension between female growth and male dominance in the black community. As Mr.--says to Celie "I never understood how you and Shug got along so well together and it bothered the hell out of me." (278) This same male confusion about women's relationships troubles Samuel in Africa as well when Nettie observes:

> This friendship among women is something Samuel,
> Corrine's husband, often talks about. Because the women
> share a husband but the husband does not share their
> friendships, it makes Samuel uneasy. (172)

The "uneasiness" and "bother" that the men speak of is the women's
ability to notice and share things about themselves that society had taught
them were not valuable or not worth noticing. This attention to their
womanhood went beyond male definition, moreover, and ultimately
demystified or even threatened the whole idea of male dominance. We see
male anxiety over women's knowledge from the first moments of the story
when Celie's stepfather appears threatened by the continued presence of
Celie in his household. Although Celie knew little of life, that which she
did know was dangerous to him. By this time she had experienced the
birth of and separation from her two children as a result of her stepfather's
incestuous behavior. It was this knowledge that he feared would inform
and empower the other girl children in the household. They would learn
through their relationship with Celie to fear and mistrust him.

> Fact is, he say, I got to git rid of her. She too old to be living
> here at home. And she a bad influence on my other girls.

We see here the very real threat posed to male domination by shared
female knowledge.

Just as the novel demonstrates the power of women sharing
experiences, it brings attention to the many women who are lost because
of the lack of friendships, family, and community. Women such as Annie
Julia were among those who were without such influences and supports.

> Nobody to talk to, nobody to visit. (21) Her family forget
> about her once she married.(127) [She] never told nobody.
> Plus, she didn't have nobody to tell.(277)

Not having anyone to share with caused her to seek other solutions to her
isolation. Annie Julia, in her search for fulfillment outside of herself and
in the arms of another man, placed her life in the control of others while
never knowing the choices to which she might aspire. Without a safe
haven in the female community, little else existed for Annie Julia: "Yeah,
say Shug, if you can't tell us, who you gon tell, God? (101)" The outcome
of her isolation and, lack of knowledge or positive influences was death.

The most powerful example of womanly assertiveness and sisterly
solidarity in *The Color Purple* is the character Sofia. Even with the
constant intrusion of the mayor's family, Sofia does not give up her beliefs
nor does she run from the perpetual battle against racism and sexism. She
makes clear her determined stance when her family thinks she might be
running away with Shug and Mary Agnes when they depart for Memphis:

> Everybody sort of cut they eyes at Sofia... It ain't me
> [leaving], she say, and her look say, Fuck you for
> entertaining the thought... But just to clear this up neat and
> quick, she say, I'm home. Period. (209)

Sofia's sense of her own value as a woman and the representative aspect
of her struggle for Celie is discussed by Angelene Jamison-Hall in her
essay "She's Just Too Womanish for Them: Alice Walker and *The Color
Purple*" where she states that:

> Sofia is one of the women who helps Celie transform
> herself from a fearful self-hating victim of male
> domination and oppression to a self-assertive and
> self-loving woman refusing to be mistreated by any man.
> Sofia shows Celie that life for women need not be
> characterized by disrespect, abuse, neglect or any other
> form of persecution.[23]

Sofia, in essence, demands her place and offers support for other women
such as Mary Agnes and others around her.

While Sofia and other women help Celie find the strength to end her
isolation and victimization, it is ultimately Shug who encourages her to
see the world in an empowered way. Delores S. Williams in her essay
"Black Women's Literature and the Task of Feminist Theology"
discusses the key role Shug plays in Celie's development when she states
that it is a transformation made possible by the "help of other Black
women who become moral agents redefining right and wrong from the
perspective of female experience" (96):

> This process involves a catalyst: a liberated, self-confident
> black woman who accelerates the movement of another
> woman away from the psychological, sexual, and
> emotional abuse that has plagued her. As she progresses
> from bondage to full moral agency, she constructs her
> notions about morality, God, sexuality, and the meaning
> of human relationships. (96-7)[24]

Williams further states that "one woman's personal growth causes
transformations in the social collective called the family" (100). It is due
to Shug's own development that she came to a point where she was no
longer concerned about constructed moral issues of right and wrong but
rather focused on self-actualization. Shug comes to see that the inhibition
of feelings she experienced in her parental home--that of a conservative
preacher--is disrespectful of creation itself. In pleasing and loving all that
God has made, she comes to believe, one loves and pleases God:

> God is everything say Shug. Everything that is or ever was
> or ever will be. And when you can feel that, and be happy
> to feel that, you've found It. (202-3)

It is the building of both understanding and love between Shug and Celie that keeps their relationship alive, transforms Celie, and allows Shug to no longer be isolated from the community. Shug becomes part of a family collective of Celie, Sofia, Albert, Harpo, Mary Agnes, and related kin and is thus able to psychologically leave the oppressive family of her birth. The novel portrays the process of reseeing one's world, coming to terms with one's identity, and thus controlling one's life as an interconnected, circular development. In the case of Celie, her world initially seemed to possess little potential for change. It was managed by silence and submission. She could not move forward or seek change since she was without knowledge of her own value. This was enforced by her inability to see clearly her past which would help explain her situation in the present. Her mother's own life, in fact, reflected the drudgery that Celie had come to accept as natural, and the result was personal stagnation. If we look at Celie's static life as a victim evolving into a circle wherein she begins to move, first around the same spot held in place by gravity, but then gradually outward in wider arcs, we see the way she transforms rootedness into freedom. The tiny circle in which she is trapped widens as the knowledge she acquires about Africa, the past, and other women propels her outward in a dance of free movement that ultimately liberates her from the gravity of psychological indoctrination. The ever-widening motion of the circle, representing personal development fueled by conscious choice, moves her to new locales and revelations of new possibilities. Once the blinders of ignorance and individual isolation are removed, Celie is able to embrace self-worth and see herself as part of a collective. Ultimately, as the novel unfolds, the circle of personal development in motion creates change and thus alters the path that both the individual and the collective may choose.

The circle of Celie's liberated self-awareness returns to or revisits the site of racialized beauty standards that is so painfully present in the novel's first section. As Celie comes to appreciate her inner worth, she realizes that the external judgments placed on her do not have to be accepted as objective truth. Indeed, she begins to realize that she has internalized these superficial standards and that it is often the image on one's *own* eyeball, placed by careful and cunning indoctrination, that distorts what one sees in the mirror and in the world. In Celie's sense of the world, it was the white man who administered life and death just as God created life and death. Seeing freedom as ordained by God and subsequently enacted as law by the words of white men, presumably made God a white man in Celie's mind.[25] "Ain't no way to read the bible and not think God white, [Shug] say... [Nettie say] It is the pictures in the bible that fool you"(202-141)."God all white too, looking like some stout white man work at the bank"(96). It was this reflection of Celie's world marred by these falsehoods that was mirrored back to her. Because god-like white men had no time to hear what a black girl might have to say and most certainly none to look on a face that possessed no signs of beauty, it is no wonder that she writes to this God: "life made you feel so ashamed you couldn't even talk about it to God, you had to write it, bad as you thought your writing was."(136) Writing, although a comfort, also silenced Celie's voice which, was a potential medium for prayer, praise, and requests for forgiveness.

It is only through looking within herself and knowledge gained from "real persons" such as Shug, that Celie is able to see God and all around her as beyond the limitations of any man's constructs of worth and beauty. When the characters in the novel begin to view each other with this awareness which is beyond social constructs of racism, they "git the man off your eyeball" (204), and their blackness is presented as rich, deeply sensual, and transcendent:

> Shug Avery was a woman. The most beautiful woman I
> ever saw. (7) She got a long pointed nose and big fleshy
> mouth. Lips look like black plum.(48) ... long black body.
> (51) [Annie Julia was] Pretty, man... Black as anything,
> and skin just as smooth. Big black eyes look like moons.
> And sweet too.(127) Harpo so black he think she [Sofia]
> bright, but she ain't that bright. Clear medium brown skin,
> gleam on it like on good furniture. (32) [Nettie in Africa
> says:]... I felt like I was seeing black for the first time. And
> Celie, there is something magical about it.(147)

The scales dropped from her eyes by the power of love Celie is able to see God's creations in their natural light, undistorted by racist, sexist hierarchies, and the magic of individual personality is revealed to her: "I think it pissed God off if you walk by the color purple in a field somewhere and don't notice it."(203) The color purple possesses the glory of the thing it graces, just as the color of one's skin contains the singular beauty of the person who is blessed with it.

Similarly, Celie comes to understand that the abusive power inflicted upon her turns against the abuser and that her own newly found power to love herself will encircle those around her as well. Donna H. Winchell in her evaluation of Celie, expresses the concept this way:

> She takes on seemingly God-like powers....As she
> confronts her husband, warning him that all the suffering
> that he has inflicted on her will be inflicted on him twofold,
> it is not her voice she hears, but the trees and the wind and
> the dirt speaking through her. In another sense, she will
> enter creation by becoming a creator herself.[26]

Her "God-like powers" as Winchell calls it, is not so much a power by which Celie becomes a creator of new life but one that comes from being one of God's creations. In confronting her husband and embracing her

own natural power, she realizes that an abusive act is ultimately against
the self since God is in all things. She tries to explain this to Mr.-- before
she leaves:

> Until you do right by me, I say, everything you even dream
> about will fail. I give it to him straight, just like it come to
> me. And it seem to come to me from the trees... Every lick
> you hit me you will suffer twice, I say. Then I say, You
> better stop talking because all I'm telling you ain't coming
> just from me. Look like when I open my mouth the air rush
> in and shape words. (213)

Here we see the circle revolving around love, not pressed downward by
the gravity of internalized self-loathing, and it takes in the natural world
as an extension of self-love and community wholeness.

Each of the female characters in *The Color Purple* revisits the world
in which she was placed and moves beyond its societal obstacles with the
help of women around her. Shug, for instance, who had been scorned by
many in the community and thus learned to be self-reliant, initially refuses
Celie's help when she is ill but eventually accepts it:

> First she say, hurry up and git finish. Then she melt down
> a little and lean back gainst my knee. That feel just right,
> she say.(55)

Sofia who defends herself well with her fists against the beatings of her
husband Harpo, similarly comes to depend on her sisters and eventually
Celie: "Just want you to know I looked to you for help." (42) As for Celie,
she writes to Nettie because the God she knows "must be sleep" and
seems not to love her back: "I don't write to God no more, I write to
you."(199) The women also come to understand that even though society
created barriers between them and judged them stereotypically, these
obstacles could be overcome by embracing their unique and unalterable
beauty.

Although the major thrust of the novel is to interrogate the double
subjugation of black women, Walker's model of human growth very much
embraces men, too, and the male characters break out of their own gender
prison. Significantly, this happens as a result of their ability to let go of
categorical thinking and role playing. Initially, the men are almost as
depersonalized as are the women despite their position of male privilege,
and it is a stance that renders them invisible. Celie, for example, sees men
initially as a collective mass for her experiences with them cause her to
shut them out: "Most times mens look pretty much alike to me."(16)
"...act just like all the other mens I know. Triflin, forgitful and
lowdown."(199) In like fashion, Mr.--, who at first sees Celie only in
terms of her utility as a target of his rage, comes to admit that he could not
bring himself to look beyond his clouded vision and embrace the human
being so evidently before him:

> Way back when you first come to live with me. You was
> so skinny, Lord, he say. And the least little thing happen,
> you looked about to fly away. You saw that, I say. I saw
> it, he said, just too big a fool to let myself care.(260)

Mr-- eventually realizes that he wants to embrace the uniqueness of all
persons instead of shutting them out as targets or servants and in so doing
shutting himself out:

> It didn't take long to realize I didn't hardly know nothing.
> And that if you ast yourself why you black or a man or a
> woman or a bush it don't mean nothing if you don't ast
> why you here, period. (289-90)

In embracing the wonders of all life and the joys of self- discovery, Mr--
claims the right and the ability to love:

> But you never know nothing more about the big things
> than you start out with. The more I wonder, he say, the
> more I love. And people start to love you back, I bet, I
> say.(290)

In the end, Mr-- is transformed into his unique identity as Albert while
Celie acknowledges the truth of the statement, "All women's [and men]
not alike .... Believe it or not. Oh, I believe it .... (59)
   The Color Purple asks us to look outward as well as inward and take
account of things in the world that are walked by, overlooked, and
unloved: "It pissed God off if you walk by the color purple in a field
somewhere and don't notice it. What it do when it pissed off? I ast. Oh, it
make something else. (203)" This color is a metaphor for Celie herself
who is weighed down by racist and sexual stereotypes that made the
essence of who she was "not noticed." She moves triumphantly in her
evolution to visibility from being a shrinking violet to a purple amaryllis
that is strong, tall, majestic, and capable of standing on its own. It is not
that the violet is not part of Celie's being but "shrinking away" from the
world has been relinquished for a powerful presence that is not only
beautiful but brings wonder to all who notice and love its color. Walker's
characters as they experience pain, knowledge, growth, and change,
"make somethin else" and strip away the disparaging labels that blind the
many who "don't notice," and they survive in spite of the intrusions of
the world that destroy, deter, and distort. Although the reclamation of
ancestry and surmounting attempts to extinguish beauty, strength,
resistance may go unrecorded in written history, works such as *The Color
Purple* attest to the continued presence of kinship, family, community,
and above all, womanly love in African American culture as unvanquished
forces for reconstructing healthy individuals and communities that pay
respect to the color...life.

Notes

1. Cary D. Wintz, *Black Culture and the Harlem Renaissance* (Houston: Rice University Press, 1988), 13. Wintz reports that "as late as 1910 Census figures show that 75 percent of American blacks lived in rural areas and that 90 percent lived in the South" (13).

2. The dominant group encompassed well-to-do whites and plantation owners, while blacks along with many poor whites suffered the brunt of economic difficulties, with the least opportunity to improve their situation. John Hope Franklin and Alfred A. Moss Jr., *From Slavery to Freedom* (New York: McGraw-Hill, 1988), 201-4.

3. Wintz, *Black*. Wintz further notes that "during the decades following the end of Reconstruction they [blacks] had witnessed the systematic erosion of the rights they had achieved under the Fourteenth and Fifteenth Amendments." (6)

4. Wintz, *Black*, 7.

5. These segregation laws mean that Nettie's teacher, Miss Beasley, is undoubtedly black, and they explain Shug's having "No place hardly to stop and really wash herself, especially her hair, on the road" (218).

6. Wintz, *Black*, 8. Lynchings, while declining in number from approximately 150 per year in the early 1890s to about half that number after 1905, continued to outrage as well as terrorize black communities. Paula Giddings notes that after the 1892 lynching of Thomas Moss, Ida B. Wells "set out to find the truth by investigating every lynching she could. All in all, she researched the circumstances of 728 lynchings that had taken place during the last decade. Her unrelenting attack on the injustice of lynchings succeeding in decreasing those numbers." Giddings, *When and Where I Enter: The Impact of Black Women on Race and Gender in America* (New York: Bantam Books, 1988), 28 and 92.

7. Paula Giddings, *When and Where I Enter*, 17-18 and 79. Giddings describes this historical incident as follows: "The lynching of March 9, 1892, was the climax of ugly events in Memphis. From the time the three Black men [Moss, McDowell, and Stewart] had gone into business for themselves, their People's Grocery, as it was called, had been the target of White resentment .... For Whites the most galling thing about the People's Grocery was that it took away business from a White store owner who had long been used to a monopoly of Black trade ... the attack came on Saturday night, when the store was full of Black men—armed Black men—who repelled the invaders and shot three Whites in the process. In short order Moss, McDowell, and Stewart were arrested along with one hundred other Blacks charged with conspiracy ... In a predawn raid, Moss, McDowell, and Stewart were taken from their cells, put on the switch engine of a train headed out of the city, and lynched." (17-18) "Racial

hostility was especially focused on Afro-Americans who had made substantial economic gains in the postwar period—gains being checked by the South's counterrevolution, the eclipse of the Freedmen's Bureau, and later the depression of 1893." (79)

8. Michele Wallace, "Blues for Mr. Spielberg," *Invisibility Blues: From Pop to Theory* (New York: Verso, 1990), 69.

9. The epistolary form that Walker uses is discussed in essays by Marjorie Pryse, "Zora Neale Hurston, Alice Walker, and the 'Ancient Power' of Black Women," *Conjuring: Black Women, Fiction, and Literary Tradition*, eds. Marjorie Pryse and Hortense J. Spillers (Bloomington: Indiana University Press, 1985), 1-23; and Emma Waters-Dawson, "From Victim to Victor: Walker's Women in *The Color Purple*," *The Aching Hearth: Family Violence in Life and Literature* (New York: Plenum Press, 1991), 255-68. Both writers conclude that Walker does not seek to validate the form as she finds it to be an expression most natural for the characters themselves.

10. Patricia Hill Collins, *Black Feminist Thought* (New York: Routledge Press, 1990), 164. I am using sex and gender the way Collins defines them. Sex is a biological category attached to the body—humans are born female or male. In contrast, gender is socially constructed. The sex/gender system consists of marking the categories of biological sex with socially constructed meanings of masculinity and femininity.

11. Zora Neale Hurston, *Their Eyes Were Watching God* (New York: Harper & Row Publishing, 1990), 14.

12. Barbara Christian, "Alice Walker: The Black Woman Artist as Wayward," *Black Feminist Criticism: Perspectives on Black Women Writers* (New York: Pergamon Press, 1985), 81-102.

13. Horrace Mann Bond, *Black American Scholars: A Study of Their Beginnings* (Detroit: Balamp Press, 1972).

14. Eugene D. Genovese, *Roll, Jordan, Roll: The World the Slaves Made* (New York: Vintage Books, 1976), 414.

15. "Is Skin Color Still a Problem in Black America?," *Ebony Magazine*, December 1984, 66-70.

16. Hazel V. Carby, *Reconstructing Womanhood: The Emergence of the Afro-American Woman Novelist* (New York: Oxford University Press, 1987), 108.

17. Wintz, *Black Culture*, 1988, 10-11. Wintz further clarifies the internalized racism that lay behind the notion that light skin as a result of miscegenation was a positive barometer not only of worth but also was a means to solving America's race problems in general: "Even anthropologist Franz Boas, who generally advocated cultural relativism, which rejected the view of Western or European cultural superiority, and

who reacted against claims that the black race as a whole was anatomically or psychologically inferior to whites, believed that black Americans were genetically inferior to whites and that only through intermarriage and the subsequent modification of the black genetic inheritance would America solve its racial problems."

18. Kathy Russell, Midge Wilson, and Ronald Hall, *Color Complex: The Politics of Skin Color Among African Americans* (New York: Anchor Books, 1992), 31.

19. Russell, et al., *The Color Complex*, 31.

20. There exists a vast amount of critical literature on the mulatto character as presented in such novels as *Iola Leroy, or Shadows Uplifted* (1895) by Frances Ellen Watkins Harper, *House Behind the Cedars* (1900) Charles Chestnutt, and writers of the Harlem Renaissance such as Nella Larsen, Jessie Fauset, Langston Hughes, etc. Critical sources are: Kimberly Wilson, "The Function of the 'Fair' Mulatto: Complexion, Audience, and Mediation in Frances Harper's *Iola Leroy*," *Cimarron Review*, January 1994, 104-13; Susan Gillman, "The Mulatto, Tragic or Triumph? The Nineteenth-Century American Race Melodrama," *The Culture of Sentiment: Race, Gender, and Sentimentality in Nineteenth-Century America* (New York: Oxford University Press, 1992), 221-43; Werner Sollors, "Never Born: The Mulatto, an American Tragedy?," *Massachusetts Review: A Quarterly of Literature*, Vol. 27, no. 2 (Summer 1986), 293-316; Dahlys Hamilton, "The Struggle of the Mulatto as Seen by Paul Green," *Paul Green's Celebration of Man, with a Bibliography*, eds. Leslie Sue Kimball and Lynn Veach Sadler (Fayetteville, NC: Human Technology Interface, Inc., 1994), 34-5.

21. These writers are discussed by Kathy Russell, Midge Wilson, and Ronald Hall, eds., *The Color Complex: The Politics of Skin Color Among African Americans* (New York: Anchor Books, 1992), 139 and Gloria T. Hull, *Color, Sex, and Poetry: Three Women Writers of the Harlem Renaissance* (Bloomington: Indiana University Press, 1987), 17.

22. Because the domestic sphere was relegated to women, the talents they possessed often went unrecognized or were devalued in their identification as successful individuals in the community. One illustration of this tendency is a book published by Monroe A. Majors, *Noted Negro Women: Their Triumphs and Activities* (New York: Books for Libraries Press, 1971). While looking for suggestions for women to include in his book, Majors was advised by Frederick Douglass that:

> We have estimable women of our variety, but not many famous ones. It is not well to claim too much for ourselves before the public. Such extravagance invites contempt rather than approval. I have thus far seen no book of importance written by a negro woman and know of no one

among use who can appropriately be called famous.
[Houston A. Baker Jr. and Charlotte Pierce-Baker,
"Patches: Quilts and Community in Alice Walker's
'Everyday Use,' " *Alice Walker: Critical Perspectives,
Past and Present,* ed. Henry Louis Gates, Jr. and K.A.
Appiah (New York: Amistad Publishing, 1993), 309-18.]

Douglass does not note the unique abilities of Phyllis Wheatley, Frances E.W. Harper, sculptor Edmonia Lewis, or Mrs. R. Douglass Sprague, women's editor of *The Washington Pilot* and daughter of the Hon. Frederick Douglass. It is well that Douglass saw the power of the individual, but to judge as not distinguished or remarkable the exemplary acts of any part of the race, in effect, diminished power for all. As Majors says on the cover page of his book: "A race, no less than a nation, is prosperous in proportion to the intelligence of its women."

23. Angelene Jamison-Hall, "She's Just Too Womanish for Them: Alice Walker and *The Color Purple,*" *Censored Books: Critical Viewpoints,* eds. Nicholas J. Karolides, Lee Burress, and John M. Kean (Metuchen, NJ: The Scarecrow Press, Inc., 1993), 191-200.

24. Delores S. Williams, "Black Women's Literature and the Task of Feminist Theology," *Immaculate and Powerful: The Female in Sacred Image and Social Reality,* eds. Clarissa W. Atkinson, Constance H. Buchanan, and Margaret R. Miles (Boston: Beacon Press, 1985), 88-110.

25. Alice Fanin, "The Pattern for Psychic Survival in *Their Eyes Were Watching God* and *The Color Purple,*" *Alice Walker and Zora Neale Hurston: The Common Bond,* ed. Lillie P. Howard (Westport, CT: Greenwood Press, 1993), 45-56. Fanin states that God is dead in Celie's eyes and that "Shug offers Celie basically Janie's philosophy of the 'spark' in all humankind as a theory about God, a theory that will finally encompass even the color purple, giving the novel its title." In my estimation God is not dead for Celie, but her sense of God, as this power exists in nature and moves through life and death, is inhibited by how she sees the world, a concept expressed in the statement "getting man off the eyeball."

26. Donna Haisty Winchell, *Alice Walker* (New York: Twayne Publishers, 1992), 93.

CHAPTER 5

Paule Marshall's *Praisesong for the Widow*

Afro-Caribbean Rituals
of Power, Place, and Identity

> Moreover, something in those small rites, an ethos they
> held in common, had reached back beyond her life and
> beyond Jay's to join them to the vast unknown lineage that
> had made their being possible. And this link, these
> connections, heard in the music and in the praisesongs of
> a Sunday: " ... I bathed in the Euphrates when dawns
> *were/young* ... ," had both protected them and put them
> in possession of a kind of power.... (137)

After reviewing the rites and ethos learned from family and community
in *Mary Prince*, the concept "rememory" or reclaiming things
remembered and things forgotten in *Beloved* by Toni Morrison, and the
need to embrace people lovingly while connecting with nature in *The
Color Purple* by Alice Walker, it is clear that rituals and traditions have
laid the foundation that keeps dispossessed African people connected.
Paule Marshall's *Praisesong for the Widow* not only reinforces these
themes but explores the sense of loss that in Marshall's mind accompanies
the substitution of material success for spiritual connection to ancestral
roots. *Praisesong*, unlike the other works examined in this study, focuses
on an urban family steeped in middle-class values, one that achieves a
piece of the American dream, but ironically, the protagonist Avey, feels
just as isolated as the downtrodden Celie in rural Georgia. Similarly, like
Sethe coping with the past traumas of enslavement, Avey must also turn
to past memories, embodied by ancestors, for a positive identity and
reliable guidance. Mary Prince's severe dislocation from family and her
legal disempowerment lead her to the same affirmation of cultural
teachings experienced by her modern, free counterpart, Avey Johnson.
These textual parallels suggest that a diasporic literature does exist for

black women bound by a striking thematic unity over time and place as well as economic circumstance. Paule Marshall's focus on a relatively affluent, independent woman, then, helps us define more clearly the special needs of black women in the New World for particular strategies of psychic survival that transcend the differences between them.

Praisesong for the Widow presents the reader with a family that by most definitions would be the all-American family. They have succeeded in moving from the economically depressed community of Harlem to the suburbs with security enough that Avey, the main character and the woman of the house, does not need to work. However, in the family's struggle to attain this status, they lose touch with the very roots of their culture and the extended family which had supported them in both spiritual and emotional ways and are being left with repressed and unfamiliar imitations of themselves. They ultimately lose much more than they gain. Avey's husband Jerome, affectionately called Jay, dies in the throes of this shallow existence, and Avey as a widow confronts the denial of her past. Usually it is the experiences of a lifetime firmly rooted in legacies that illuminate where one has come from, but for Avey the pretense of experience, the inhibition of expression, and the relinquishing of culture and tradition leave her mind clouded and disconnected from the very forces that would help define who she is.

Avey and Jay Johnson buy into the American dream created by whites, but ultimately find it to be a destructive force in their lives that requires abandonment of identity and culture.[1] Their movement from poverty in Harlem to middle-class security in suburbia is accompanied significantly by gradual abandonment of cultural rituals that initially sustain them. The more they progress materially, therefore, the farther they go from the things that nourish identity. One example of this paradoxical dynamic is Jay's reliance on African American music in the early years of their marriage to ease the continual exploitation he endured at his various jobs. Music took away the suppressed rage provoked by racism on the job and made it possible for him to be whole and happy for his family. Every day without fail Jay would come home, put a record on the phonograph before he did anything else, and let the music wash away the struggles of the day:

> Until gradually, under their ministrations, the fatigue and
> strain of the long day spent doing the two jobs—his and
> his boss's would ease from his face, and his body ....(94)

On the most difficult of days, he would return home and play blues records, not even stopping to take off his coat or sit down until he could untie the knots in his spirit. Emphasizing the spirituality of music, the narrative foregrounds the family's pleasant breakfasts together on Sundays while listening to spirituals on the radio as backdrop for a cherished routine. Other examples of cultural rituals observed by the family included Jay's recitation of poetry by Langston Hughes accompanied by hand gestures to emphasize the words for the amusement of their oldest daughter, Sis. Perhaps the most important ritual binding the family to a strong cultural heritage was the yearly trip they would take to Tatem where Great-aunt Cuney had lived. There Avey would share with Jay Great-aunt Cuney's story of the Ibo people, who, after arriving on the Georgia shore, rejected slavery and walked back home across the water.

Competing with these rituals of affirmation adopted to deal with the stresses of their economic marginality are the very real dangers that beset people in Harlem. A location of cultural identity and pride, Harlem is also a place where people suffer material deprivation and family disintegration, a specter that haunts the Johnsons and ultimately hardens their determination to leave it behind. The primary symbol of Harlem's destructive side is the weekend ritual of nightmarish proportion enacted by the half-crazed neighbor of the Johnsons who goes looking for her philandering husband and leaves her children unattended. The narrative connects this woman's desperation with the Harlem milieu that threatens to envelop everyone on Halsey Street:

> Her rage those dark mornings spoke not only for herself but for the thousands like her for blocks around, lying sleepless in the cold-water flats and one-room kitchenettes .... (108)

Avey understood her neighbor's crazed actions for she, too, was consumed by anxiety every time Jay worked late nights and she feared his being unfaithful to her. Pregnant with their third child, Avey was aware of the continual battle to survive and recognized the formula for family disintegration that could turn her into a desperate wife and mother and Jay into a wayward husband. Jay, too, felt the strain of marginal living and during a pivotal argument with Avey, on a cold winter night, articulates the fatal choice he feels he must make between identification with his heritage and getting away from the dangers of Harlem. Not wanting to become like his neighbors on Halsey Street, Jay confuses their distress with values he has absorbed from the dominant culture which blame them for their plight. Blind to the fact that he has spiritual resources many others do not for coping with racism, Jay distances himself from "those Negroes" who cannot alleviate their suffering enough to lead stable lives:

> "If they'd just cut out all the good-timing and get down to some hard work, put their minds to something, they'd get somewhere." Holding them solely responsible. When she reminded him of the countless times he had been refused work despite all his efforts ... [he replied] "we need to work and build our own, to have our own. Our own! Our own!" ... Lashing out periodically at her, himself, and at that world which had repeatedly denied him ....(135)

Adopting the individualistic perspective of a white success story, Jay fatally divorces himself from the very racial identity that sustained him through hardship and embraces the white American dream as the whole of his vision.

Important to Marshall's novel are the choices the characters make when faced with an economic and social system that is exclusive, restrictive, and racist, one that establishes barriers to one's growth. Jerome Johnson's choice is to work within this limiting system and to focus his energies toward gaining material success but little else:

> Even things that had once been important to him, that he needed, such as the music, the old blues records that had restored him at the end of the day, found themselves abandoned on the sidelines, out of his line of vision.(115)

When he succeeds in opening his own accounting service, Jerome moves his family from Halsey Street with its black rhythms and cadences to the aptly named suburb of White Plains, New York. Symbolically erasing his aesthetic side, Jay removes his cherished mustache as well at this point with a pointed remark about its uselessness: "Damn thing was getting to be a nuisance. You'll soon get used to me without it" (131). Jay's transformation into a more colorless figure is astutely recognized by Avey who sees the man of their early years slipping away. Of the vanished mustache, for instance, she reflects: "With the mustache no longer there it seemed that the last trace of everything that was distinctive and special about him had vanished also" (131). She begins to visualize a double face for Jay who now adopts his formal name. Jerome, one that resembles him but that is "pale and shadowy."(132)

The repression of Jay Johnson is the price he pays for moving to an affluent neighborhood in postwar America, and Avey, as a suburban housewife, is inevitably drawn into his metamorphosis: "They [Jerome and Avey] were getting to look, even to sound alike ...." (141) Gradually Avey, too, sacrifices the unique aspects of herself rooted in her African heritage such as her full lips that she now keeps pulled in. As Barbara Christian notes: "that held-in lip had become a permanent part of her expression over the years"(28).[2] Ultimately, Jerome Johnson's pursuit of the American dream costs him his physical as well as his spiritual life when the rage he suppresses and the silence that marks his cultural disinheritance turn inward, resulting in a cerebral hemorrhage: " finally the confusion, contradiction and rage of it all sent the blood flooding his brain one night as he slept in the bed next to hers" (135). Avey Johnson's family has become the embodiment of American success but at the cost of its African American identity.

In dramatic contrast to the choice made by Jerome Johnson for his family's survival is the detailed attention given in the novel to Avey's Great-aunt Cuney's choices in Tatem. Central to Avey's memory of her Great-aunt is the mythological site of Ibo Landing where she was taken during annual summer visits. Located where the waters around Tatem and the open sea meet, this place was referred to only as "The Landing" by people in Tatem, but Great-aunt Cuney insisted on preserving its full name in order not to erase the memory of the African people after whom it was named. On every visit Great-aunt Cuney would ritualistically travel the same path to Ibo Landing with Avey, and once there she would always tell the story of the Ibos in precisely the same manner. This legend, which was relayed to Great-aunt Cuney by her gran', chronicles the Ibos' journey from Africa. Having the clairvoyant ability to see what was in store for them in the New World, these Ibos took destiny into their own hands and, undaunted by the ocean that separated them from Africa, picked up their chains, broke into song, and walked on top of the water back to their homeland.

The tale of Ibo Landing, which preserves a mythological moment during slavery, is Great-aunt Cuney's legacy to Avey, one that conveys the possibility of choice even in a powerless condition, and it encourages Avey to shape her own identity and act on her desires. Whether or not the Ibos actually walked on water is of no concern to Great-aunt Cuney, for once they turned their backs on slavery, they exercised a control over their own lives that was denied black people for centuries. It symbolizes for her the idea that dispossessed people can put the spirit and body beyond the white man's control if they believe in something greater than a manmade social/economic system. Great-aunt Cuney articulates the power of such a force that exceeds historically bound institutions when she says to Avey:

> Now you wouldna thought they'd of got very far seeing as it was water they was walking on. Besides they had all that iron on 'em. Iron on they ankles and they wrists and fastened 'round they necks like a dog collar. 'Nuff iron to sink an army…. But chains didn't stop those Ibos none…. Left the white folks standin' back here with they mouth hung open and they taken off down the river on foot. Stepping.(38-39)

It is the right to choose, being true to self in spite of the white man's definition of destiny, sin, or nature that makes Great-aunt Cuney feel "her body … might be in Tatem but her mind was long gone with the Ibos…."(39)

Reinforcing the story's ritual power for Avey is the way in which Great-aunt Cuney personifies the legend through her own journey toward self-actualization. Paralleling in some ways Avey's assimilation of values constructed by white people, Great-aunt Cuney's membership in a local church in part separates her from the African rituals it has distorted as a result of slavery. Central to this notion of distortion is Marshall's foregrounding of the ringshout, a ritual for church members to move and sing in a circle to praise God. The narrative description of the ringshout alludes to its complex origins as a Christian adaptation of African dance rituals:[3]

> Through the open door the handful of elderly men and women ... could be seen slowly circling in a loose ring ... with a beat that was as precise and intricate as a drums. They ... used their hands as racing tambourines, slapped their knees and thighs and chest in dazzling syncopated rhythm. They worked their shoulders; even succeeded at giving a mean roll of their aged hips... yet their feet never once left the floor or, worse, crossed each other in a dance step ... (34)

It is during one such gathering at the church that the contradictions of the ringshout come to the surface and Great-aunt Cuney is accused of letting her feet cross, an act that was considered dancing and thus a sin and illegal under the white man's law.[4] Evicted from the church for one day, Great-aunt Cuney, who was initially confused as to why this negative reaction accompanied her spirit-filled worship, left forever, never to return as a member of this group. Wrenched from the church by its upholding of a rule that forbids African tradition, Great-aunt Cuney comes to question much that she has accepted automatically and turns instead to her Ibo ancestry for guidance and meaning.

Illustrating how impossible it is to turn away completely from her mixed heritage as an African American, however, Great-aunt Cuney continues to watch the ringshout ritual even after she leaves the church.[5] She could not totally abandon this ritual, for it had been a part of the legacy through which blacks survived and maintained at least some aspects of their culture.[6] What Great-aunt Cuney had come to see was that the stories and traditions of her African ancestors, specifically those that were passed down to her by her gran' Avatara, had a most profound impact on her life and should not be suppressed any longer. She is challenged then to incorporate them into her other cultural heritage as an Americanized black woman and to find a way to blend Christianity with African legacies. One instance where she is able to do this is when Avey asks why the Ibos did not drown when they walked across the water:

> "Did it say Jesus drowned when he went walking on the water in that Sunday School book your momma always sends with you?" "No, ma'am." "I din' think so. You got any more questions?" She [Avey] had shaken her head "no." (40)

Just as Christianity asks one to believe in Jesus and the extraordinary power of love he demonstrated, it goes without question in Great-aunt Cuney's mind that the story of the Ibos deserves the same respect, for it too represents vital lessons about life and death. In equating the two legends, she succeeds in demystifying Christian mythology as the only

valid spiritual form of reference for Avey. Similarly, Great-aunt Cuney
values the ringshout as a descendant of African dancing outlawed by
slaveowners who were outwitted by the tempering of traditional dance
movements into a Christian ritual. At the same time, she rejects the law
itself and resists the prohibition against dancing as an attempt to erase a
valid religious and cultural tradition. Embracing the Ibo as her root
ancestry, which is connected to a pure African legacy, allows Great-aunt
Cuney to stand outside her community while not becoming alienated from
her racial identity.

The memory of Great-aunt Cuney's legendary story about Ibo
Landing and her response to her church's ringshout ritual would prove
instrumental in Avey's evolution from her own entrapped or coopted
identity as a modern American woman to a more authentic affirmation of
her racial heritage. This evolutionary journey begins, metaphorically, on
board a cruise ship in the Caribbean with her friends when Avey is into
the third year of her widowhood, the scene which is actually our narrative
introduction to Avey. Participating in a leisure ritual of middle-class life,
an elaborate dinner, Avey reaches a moment of epiphany when she is
presented with dessert--a parfait. Arrested by the image of women in a
mirror hung in the dining hall, Avey is startled to realize that she is among
them but cannot see herself:

> But for a long confused moment Avey Johnson could not
> place the woman in beige crepe de Chine and pearls seated
> with them ... The parfait, a long-handled spoon beside it,
> was sitting waiting for her on the table as she turned away,
> frowning slightly, from the reflection in the mirror. Oddly
> enough there was not nausea or pain, ... only the
> mysterious clogged and swollen feeling which differed in
> intensity and came and went at will. (48-52)

Once she realizes she is looking directly at her own reflection, Avey is so
unnerved that she cannot eat the parfait for which she has denied herself
all previous treats of the meal. The reward of the parfait represents, of
course, the delayed gratification undergirding middle-class values, just as
the repression of Avey's own identity and the squelching of her desire to
reach out to others of her culture were rewarded with a middle-class life.
Neither the parfait nor the middle-class existence seem adequate anymore
to compensate for what she has lost.

This feeling of disorientation continues well into the next day as Avey
moves through the ship in a daze seeking refuge from the uncomfortable
feelings that consume her. As Avey's friends, Thomasina and Clarice,
learn that she will leave the ship, they too question the identity of this
woman whom they thought so rational and steeped in the values they
themselves possessed:

> Could it be [Thomasina] had misread her all these years
> and there was more to her than she suspected: a force, a

fire beneath that reserved exterior that was not to be trifled
with? Her wondering gaze focused on the underlip which
was still slightly pursed to reveal the no-nonsense edging
of pink she had never seen before.(62)

The soft pink of Avey's lips to which this passage refers could only be
seen due to an easing of the physical repression which had narrowed her
full lips, a familiar feature among people with African ancestry.
Thomasina, who had never seen this aspect of Avey before, immediately
wants to reject it. Avey thus becomes so unfamiliar to her friends that her
behavior suggests to them one who is unstable, stressed, and suffering
from a psychic breach with reality.⁷ What they see in truth is the
emergence of an Avey they do not know, just as they do not know their
own authentic identity, but one who has to be consciously reclaimed for
her psychic survival.

To find herself, Avey must seal herself off from these friends whose
lives mirror her own engulfed state, just as the crazed neighbor on Halsey
Street reflected the dangers of poverty. She must descend into isolation
and chaos before she can reconstruct a self based on the truth of who she
is. Instrumental to this re-discovery is a dream she has about Great-aunt
Cuney forcing Avey to Ibo Landing. In the dream Avey finds herself being
angry and doing all she can not to go. Great-aunt Cuney grasps Avey
firmly by the arm, however, and pulls her along saying, "Come/won't you
come"(44), but Avey's continued resistance causes them to engage in a
brawling, clothes-tearing battle. Avey's effort to resist her Great-aunt
Cuney in the dream results, significantly, in purposeless flailing about in
the cruise ship stateroom leaving her emotionally and physically
exhausted. The story Avey cannot bear to hear in the dream originates
from Avey's namesake Avatara, but because she is not yet ready to reclaim
that connection, Avey resists her Great-aunt's spiritual legacy. As Gay
Wilentz notes, it is the continuing presence of Great-aunt Cuney in Avey's
life, even as a dream, that makes the murky past a potent element of the
present:

> Although Avey is helped by Lebert Joseph and the old
> matrons of the island, the guiding force is Great-aunt
> Cuney. It is also pertinent that during Avey's stay in the
> Caribbean, many of the old and young women as well as
> Joseph himself function as personae for Great-aunt
> Cuney... she also acts as a presence for the reader, so that
> we are constantly super-imposing a Tatem and the
> African-American experience over the Afro-Caribbean
> scene.⁸

It is primarily a connection to women, therefore, that Avey needs to
reconstruct and substitute for the problematic relationships she has
experienced within the middle-class contemporary world.

Startled out of her middle-class complacency by the visions that begin to come to her, Avey is oppressed by the excess of activities in her life that have no substance. Moreover, she begins to experience all that she has previously repressed in order to appear in control of her fate: the failure to mourn the loss of *Jay* Johnson, not *Jerome* Johnson; the inadequate attention paid to the past and to others who were still struggling as she and Jay had struggled; the fact that in squeezing tightly to the American dream, she and Jay had arrogantly set themselves as a race apart; and the knowledge of all they had sacrificed for "too much" of the wrong things.[9] As the repression of so many painful realities fades away, Avey experiences a cleansing release of rage:

> [She saw the] outline of another face superimposed on hers like a second skin, a thin-lipped stranger's face, alive and mocking ... Over and over, in a rage of tears, she assaulted the dark and empty air, trying with each blow to get at the derisive face. (142)

As in a ritualistic cleansing, Avey finds her mind "emptied of the contents of the past thirty years during the night, so that she had awakened with it like a slate that had been wiped clean, a *tabula rasa* upon which a whole new history could be written"(151). After her catharsis, Avey no longer restrains her body with girdles or conformist coordinated suits and accessories but wears loose-fitting clothes. This is an important freeing step, of course, but the wrinkled condition of her clothes and her half-combed hair reflect the internal disarray that continues to trouble her. She needs desperately to release aspects of herself that have long been silenced or hidden and to shed the external mask that was a middle-class, middle-aged woman, but in order to do that, Avey must bring the wisdom of her Great-aunt out of her dreams and into the world as she knows it. She must find ways to connect with a living heritage.

Barbara Christian in her essay, "Trajectories of Self-Definition," makes note of Marshall's attempt to demonstrate that African legacies such as the ones Avey seeks are very much present in the contemporary world:

> Marshall concentrates, more than any of the other novelists of this period, on delineating the essential African wisdom still alive in New World black communities.[10]

This is an important point because it asserts that knowledge found in ancestral experiences is not only a function of historical memory as passed down from generation to generation, but also of current cultural practice that is available firsthand from those who are still alive. People of the diaspora can learn much from the living elders of their communities whose physical presence is a testament of their ability to survive and endure. Recognizing the conscious commitment of "Old Parents" and "The Long-time Peoples" to the future as well as to the confraternity of Africans provides a basis for understanding one's place in the world. Avey must come to see, then, that modern life has not replaced African old-world traditions, which are still alive and vibrant. She must come to realize that shedding her middle-class accoutrements is only the first step in a journey that is both backward and lateral.

The portion of Avey's journey that occurs on Grenada emphasizes the long spiritual path she must walk if she is to retrieve her African identity, and it begins with her accidental encounter with an unrecognizable elder, an Out-islander named Lebert Joseph. He is among the oldest of the generations of Africans from a nation called the Chamba. Avey, due to her years of absence from cultural and family traditions, is at a loss, of course, as to her nation or tribal origins. She cannot even begin to answer the question that Lebert Joseph asks her when she takes refuge from the heat in his shack while walking along the beach before her flight to New York: "And what you is?"(166) She searches her thoughts until she comes to the place where her house and recent memories reside--North White Plains, New York:

> "I plan on being home tonight, in my own house ..." She
> faltered at the word 'house,' seeing projected suddenly on
> the blank screen of her mind ... and suddenly, at the
> thought of ... North White Plains, there it was again; the
> peculiar and bloated feeling in her stomach and under her
> heart ... (181)

Joseph is saddened by Avey's lack of knowledge about her nation, but once she does respond knowledgably to the mention of the Juba dance, he comes to see Avey as representative of the members of his own family who have lost touch with the old rituals and traditions. He therefore invites her to go on the Carriacou Excursion which is based on an actual annual ritual in Grenada when Out-islanders like Lebert Joseph return to see family, reminisce, and reconnect with family traditions.[11] Joseph encourages Avey to embrace the welcome that is always there for her on Carriacou and others who are lost, and his words echo those of Great-aunt Cuney in Avey's dream:

> "You must come." And although the man had never once
> touched her, she felt as if he had reached out and taken her
> gently but firmly now by the wrist.(183)

Avey's crossing the water to Carriacou from Grenada is the central ritual of the novel and alludes to an old African ritual in which ancestors are deified.[12] Never having experienced this type of travel before, Avey becomes violently ill, regurgitating continuously until her stomach is completely empty. In this way, she purges herself of the clogged and swollen feeling that came with every thought of her New York home, the fear of and discomfort with her own reflection, and the rage that she had repressed for so long. She becomes so sick that she, like others on the boat who are making the trip for the first time, has to be taken below to rest. Although she is engulfed by nausea, Avey's awareness of the other black people on this voyage who are similarly afflicted breaks through her awful isolation and allows her to tolerate the disorientation. The isolation from her past is destroyed as well for she senses herself, in an almost dream-like state, as a reflection of her ancestors who as slaves crossed these waters.[13]

> She was alone in the deckhouse .... Yet she had the impression of ... other bodies lying crowded in with her in the hot, airless dark. A multitude it felt like lay packed around her in the filth and stench of themselves, just as she was. Their moans, rising and falling with each rise and plunge of the schooner .... Their suffering — the depth of it, the weight of it in the cramped — made hers of no consequence. (209)

She realizes out of respect for her ancestors' suffering that hers is of no consequence. It is their suffering that creates the meaning behind the rituals and the traditions that she is preparing to embrace, and it is this same respect for those ancestors that keeps the excursion alive.

There is a third, more important, isolation that is breached in this scene, however, as the old women on the boat whom Avey sits among care for her when she is ill:

> With Lebert Joseph quickly clearing a path for them, the two old women half-lead, half-carried her--barely conscious and with her hands over her face--through the crowd over to the small deckhouse midship. They had read her look the moment she leaped up with the silent scream and had acted.(208)

Athena Vrettos provides insight about the healing role of these old women in her essay, "Curative Domains: Women, Healing and History in Black Women's Narratives":

> They shield her body and provide a chorus to her heaving, exclaiming "Bon" with every lump she disgorges. Their healing is itself an act of communication as they whisper soothingly in her ear and hold her to counter the boat's rocking.[14]

The soothing caretaking Vrettos describes recalls the musical rhythms that had eased Jay and Avey in their earlier life, the powerful "Amens" of her own mother's church which she had forgotten, and Avey's experiences with Great-aunt Cuney listening to the ringshout.

Joseph's daughter, Rosalie Parvay, continues the female caretaking when Avey arrives at the island and is taken to Rosalie's home. There, she cares for Avey as tenderly as one would a child when she is ritually washed, rubbed, and oiled to bring life and strength back to her body.

> They entered the bedroom in a procession of two, Rosalie
> Parvay in front ... the closed-faced maid looming tall
> behind her.... For a long while there was silence in the room
> ... — she not only oiled and kneaded them [Avey's limbs]
> thoroughly, but afterwards proceeded to stretch them.... It
> was the way Avey Johnson used to stretch the limbs of her
> children after giving them their baths when they were
> infants. To see to it that their bones grew straight.
> (218-222)

It is the ritual of the bath that brings back forgotten memories of her
mother's nurturing powers and, by extension, those of all black women:
"The memory took over, and for long minutes she was the child in the
washtub again" (221).[15] Rosalie also (re)creates the music of healing in
a "curious slightly audible singsong"(220) which "could be heard in the
remotest corners of her [Avey's] body. 'Bon'" (224). These women
working together represent the importance and the power of the female
community, along with the African rituals of their culture, in providing
the support that encourages the healing as well as wholeness that Avey
seeks. It is only, in fact, when Avey feels this soothing bond with other
living black women that she can embrace herself as a tangible, sensual
human being with a secure place in contemporary life.

The final ritual that reconnects Avey to the elements of her culture
that will help give direction to her life is the dance of nations. Abena P.
Busia, in her essay "What Is Your Nation?", agrees with the idea that up
to this point the events of Avey's trip have been preparation for the
reclamation that she is ready to make:

> Everything that has happened to the widow since her
> meeting with Lebert Joseph has been a ritual preparation
> for this moment; she has been prepared spiritually through
> the ordeals of her two dreams, of Jerome and Great-aunt
> Cuney, and her recognition of her spiritual orphanage; she
> has been prepared physically by being purged on the sea
> voyage, by vomiting and excreting everything inside her;
> and she has been prepared ritually and reminded of the
> essential unity of the body and the soul by being bathed in
> absolution like a supplicant by Lebert Joseph's daughter
> Rosalie Parvay. It is at the festival that we perceive the
> significance of all the various folk motifs that have run
> through the text.[16]

It is thus the nation dance that is the culmination of Avey's journey and
helps to send her back into the world having reclaimed her cultural wealth,
connected to and focused on what her role in life should be.

Before she can participate in this ritual, however, Avey must be
reintegrated into her lost ancestral heritage by being a part of the Beg
Pardon dance which offers respect to ancestors for the generations who
are unable to participate in the dance. The Beg Pardon dance is a crucial

part of Avey's island experience, for it proclaims that all are able to return to the celebration of ancestors, rituals, and traditions even after being lost. Even though she may not have been fully aware of ancestral traditions in her modern American life, Avey has been connected to them through her memory of family rituals and even through the personal upheaval she has allowed herself to undergo. Therefore she is receptive to the ritual dance of reclamation know as the Beg Pardon.

After symbolically reconnecting with her ancestors in this way, Avey is ready to take part in the nation dance. She watches as each person comes to represent their nation and to dance the steps that time has altered, but for which the spirit and meaning remain strong. The muted movements so engage Avey that she can sense the respect of the dancers for what they are doing: "The restraint and understatement in the dancing, which was not even really dancing, the deflected emotion in the voices were somehow right. It was the essence of something rather than the thing itself she was witnessing"(240). This "essence" that she perceived was reminiscent of what Avey felt when Great-aunt Cuney would stop on the roadside in Tatem and watch the church folk perform the altered but nevertheless African-inspired ringshout. After watching the Carriacou dancers for some time Avey takes to her feet and dances the way she remembers the ringshout moving, careful not to cross her feet. Just as she embraces the one ritual dance that she has watched in her childhood, so does each person in the yard of Lebert Joseph bring a part of their nation to the celebration. Even the elders, it is made clear, have valuable roles:

> And in sober counterpoint to the jump-up [the dance of the
> young people], they were performing the rhythmic trudge
> that couldn't be called dancing, yet at the same time was
> something more than merely walking. A non-dance
> designed to conserve their failing strength and see them
> through the night. Occasionally, even they forgot
> themselves and a hip for all its stiffness would swing out.
> (246)

At first glance, Avey's performance of the ringshout dance appears to negate her Great-aunt Cuney's rebellious affirmation of African traditions, but I think there are key contextual differences that do not encourage such an interpretation. First, Avey is exercising her right to present herself as she pleases whereas Great-aunt Cuney was denied that right. Moreover, Great-aunt Cuney had moved beyond the reason for which the non-dance of the ringshout was created toward a greater sense of worship that embraced African rituals and traditions more fully. Avey, on the other hand, did the non-dance of the ringshout to show respect for those ancestors who went before her and survived while subtly confronting white law and religion. The difference also lies in the fact that Avey was incorporating the dance of the ringshout--a part of African

American Christian worship--into the dance of the Carriacou--a part of an
African Caribbean celebration. Carol Boyce Davies sheds light on Avey's
act when she describes the nation dance as: "A documented ritual
enactment of Pan-African unity and therefore [it] represents the coming
together of all those of the African diaspora."[17] The wholeness that
evolves out of this experience for Avey brings together the aspects of her
individuality as a woman, an African American, and a member of the
Pan-African community. In engaging her childhood memories of
Great-aunt Cuney through the ringshout dance, Avey discovers
connections and gains understanding about the past that extend far beyond
mere nostalgia for a lost time. Angelita Reyes, in her essay "Carnival as
an Archaeological Site for Memory," looks at the Carriacou excursion as
invoking the memory of place specifically, one that transforms Avey from
a disembodied traveler to a woman with roots:

> By going to Carriacou and experiencing the ritual
> performance of New World African dancing and
> drumming, Avey Johnson rediscovers her own memory of
> place as an American of African ancestry. When she leaves
> Carriacou, she resolves to renew her ties with her own
> archaeological site of memory in Tatem, South Carolina.[18]

Avey also comes away from Carriacou with the songs of women in
her ear as well as the music of black people abandoned by her and her
husband as they climbed the economic ladder. Abena Busia expounds on
the meaning of song to Avey's reclamation process when she explains
what the title's reference to praisesong signifies:

> the history, myths and legends of a whole people or their
> representatives and can be used to celebrate communal
> triumph or the greatness of rulers and the nobility of the
> valiant and brave, whether in life or death ... [it is]sung
> to mark social transition. [It is] sung as a part of rites of
> passage that mark the upward movement of a person from
> one group to the next.[19]

Avey is thus part of a communal victory over attempted erasure of her
people and becomes one of the noble, valiant, and brave who have the
courage to metamorphose into a more evolved identity, one that embraces
a pain-filled past. This is a narrative of praisesong for the widow Johnson
who leaves the false island of an American cruise ship for the vibrant
island of dance and song that protected African traditions in the New
World.
       Marshall's novel, then, ends as the celebration of a new consciousness
that moves Avey forward in life and affirms that it has not been lost in the
midst of a consumerism based on white visions of success. In fact, the

novel implies, it is possible to combine material comforts with African-inspired traditions and solid memories of old world customs:

> Would it have been possible to have done both? That is, to have wrested, as they had done over all those years, the means needed to rescue them from Halsey Street and to see the children through, while preserving, safeguarding, treasuring those things that had come down to them over the generations, which had defined them in a particular way. The most vivid, the most valuable part of themselves! They could have done both ....(139)

The Johnsons' tragic mistake was having embraced the American dream as the whole of their vision while ignoring the cultural price it would exact. The dream does not provide solid traditions for people of color, Avey discovers, nor does it teach African Americans to survive in a society that despises them. As Avey discovers the outer limits of her self-alienation, she realizes it is the neighbor woman and her family on Halsey Street who should not be forgotten even though they are not to be emulated either; it is Great-aunt Cuney's story of the Ibos' determination to escape slavery that is to be remembered and learned from; it is the trips to Tatem and the family's Sunday rituals that are a refuge against racism, providing time to reflect about the past in meaningful, self-affirming ways. Once the lessons and emotional healing that African-inspired rituals and traditions offered were lost, the Johnsons' lives were consumed with such destructiveness that the self was left disoriented and angry. Although financially successful, the happiness that this vision of the American dream promised the Johnsons, therefore, was not theirs to claim.

It is important to note that the history of Caribbean slavery is an important element of *Praisesong for the Widow* just as it was of Mary Prince's narrative, because the strength of African ancestral traditions and rituals there was so much greater than in the United States due to the dynamic of oppression in that region. Both Mary Prince, the historical slave, and Avey Johnson, the fictional modern free woman, were dramatically influenced by family teachings, those who had strong ties with their homeland, and living examples of those who had resisted slavery successfully. As Paule Marshall has demonstrated, positive factors which shaped a confrontational stance for the Caribbean slave and helped preserve cultural practices are still operating today there despite intense poverty, to make possible the recovery of important African roots for African Americans.

At the same time, although rituals of the Caribbean such as the Carriacou Excursion reflect its more secure ties to African origins, Marshall makes clear that slavery's legacy of racist dehumanization is shared by all members of the diaspora in a world that continues to be dominated by whites. Slavery dispersed communities in ways that make cultural practices hard to preserve and, therefore, the unity which relies on them is also difficult to preserve. What is inspirational about Marshall's message is that slavery's disruption of bonding rituals need not be irrevocable. Even for dispossessed Africans in the contemporary United States who are far removed from ancestral memory and atomized by the mirage of the American dream, retrieval of a diasporic identity is still possible. The siren song of material gain does not have to be the only music heard by African Americans like Avey Johnson. Praisesong still exists and is freely given to those who open themselves to its healing properties. Avey overcomes the rage and silence that kill her husband, the alienation from her body's African rhythms that nearly kills her soul, through the courage to seek the wisdom of Caribbean islanders, poor in a material sense but rich in spiritual resources. She stands as a reminder that as people of the diaspora gain access to white society, they must be careful not to lose "too much" as they struggle with the rage and isolation that comes from a cultural void. Identity, place, and personal power are the gifts Avey receives from the people of Carriacou, just as her foremother, Mary Prince, received them from the inhabitants of Turk's Island. They are precious jewels, Paule Marshall implies, that were wisely hoarded in the Caribbean through ancient reservoirs of recall much stronger than the iron bands of economic or political power. She, like other women of the diaspora, has African dance in her step and praisesong in her heart if only she will allow herself the healing touch of communal embrace. For all her modern urban sophistication, it is only through the reclamation of rituals and traditions in which the essence of African wisdom is passed on that Avey Johnson can reconnect her mind, body, and spirit while directing herself toward a secure sense of identity, place, and power.

Notes

1. Other texts that interrogate the possibilities of the American dream for African Americans include novels such as *The Invisible Man* by Ralph Ellison, *Passing* by Nella Larsen, *Native Son* by Richard Wright, and *Plum Bun* by Jessie Fauset, to name a very few.

2. Barbara Christian, "Trajectories of Self-Definition," *Conjuring: Black Women, Fiction, and Literary Tradition*, eds. Marjorie Pryse and Hortense J. Spillers (Bloomington: Indiana University Press, 1985), 233-48. Christian also notes that "Paule Marshall also focuses on the dangers of materialism, on how the fear of poverty and failure has affected Avey's and Jay Johnson's marriage--and their sense of themselves as black--to such an extent that they do not even recognize own their own faces. *Praisesong* has, as one of its major themes, middle-aged, middle-class Avey Johnson's journey back to herself, an essential part of which is the African wisdom still alive in the rituals of black societies in the West." (245)

3. The ringshout was created by Africans to bring elements of African culture into their conversion to Christianity. It is particularly important as a legacy for blacks because it preserves an engagement with African culture that was in the majority of cases denied them. Eugene D. Genovese, *Roll, Jordan, Roll: The World the Slaves Made* (New York: Vintage Books, 1976, 233-34.

4. Although the ringshout sought to incorporate some practices of African culture, such as dancing and other movements, into Christian worship, these practices were ultimately recognized as a threat to the colonial plan of oppression. Michael Mullin describes the ways the ringshout was presented in reports written by Methodists who complained of spirit-filled conversions: "'The spirit descending,' while struggling to contain the slaves' [produced] profound excited reactions to an event blacks understood so well.... In South Carolina, where new Negroes were numerous and slaves overall were not assimilated, conversion for a while threatened to ignite serious resistance. In time, however, as the evangelicals assumed control of the slaves' leisure to the extent of stifling dancing and the rituals it generated, resistance was negligible until the Civil War." Michael Mullin, *Africa in America: Slave Acculturation and Resistance in the American South and the British Caribbean 1736-1831* (Chicago: University of Illinois Press, 1994), 199-211. In order to control behavior and prevent reconnection with cultural ideas and practices from their homeland, dancing was deemed illegal for slaves. It was the rejection of African dancing by Christians as a continuation of oppression that caused Great-Aunt Cuney to question and then leave the church.

5. Genovese, *Roll, Jordan, Roll*, 233-34.

6. Michael Mullin argues that the ringshout preserved vital aspects of African culture and rejects the notion that conversion to Christianity was another form of the planter's hegemonic control of slave life: "A resistance reply to this damaging argument is that such slave innovations as spirituals, the shout, and counterclockwise shuffle dance demontrated an Africanized Christianity--'the invisible religion'--that formed the base for the considerable cultural autonomy blacks achieved in antebellum slave quarters." *Africa in America*, 174-75.

7. Literature that addresses a female breach with reality or madness is explored by Lillian Feder, *Madness in Literature* (Princeton University Press, 1980); Sandra Gilbert and Susan Guban, *Madwoman in the Attic: The Woman Writer and the Nineteenth Century Literary Imagination* (New Haven: Yale University Press, 1970); Evelyn O'Callaghan, "Interior Schisms Dramatized: The Treatment of the 'Mad' Woman in the Work of Some Female Caribbean Novelists," *Out of Kumbla: Caribbean Women and Literature*, eds. Carole Boyce Davies and Elaine Savory Fido (Trenton, NJ: African World Press, Inc., 1994), 89-109.

8. Gay Wilentz, "Towards a Spiritual Middle Passage Back: Paule Marshall's Diasporic Vision in *Praisesong for the Widow*," *Obsidian II*, Vol. 5, no. 3 (Winter 1990, 13).

9. Loudell F. Snow, *Walkin over Medicine* (Boulder: Westview Press, 1993), 67-94, interrogates the myth that possessions bring happiness, a myth that Avey accepts all too completely: "The acquisition of nice things is valued; accumulation of too much, however, invites divine displeasure or the envy of a neighbor. Unfortunately, the fine line between 'not enough' and 'too much' is not always easy to assess or maintain. One must always be vigilant," 244.

10. Christian, "Trajectories," 244.

11. The nation to which one was connected in Africa has been remembered and carried forward from generation to generation on the island of Carriacou. Many people know from what group in Africa they have come, while sharing a respect for all groups who survived against the difficult times of slavery and subjugation. National origins of blacks during slavery were not recognized in all areas of colonization but were in certain areas of the Americas and the Caribbean used to delineate group characteristics and temperament. As a general rule, newly arrived Africans were called "New Negroes," but more specific designations of origin also were mentioned. Michael Mullin in *Africa in America* goes into careful detail regarding the various uses of origins and ethnicity for the slave in the New World and the Caribbean; "In Jamaica, and for a while in South Carolina, whites occasionally used "nation" in place of country (Africa) . . . . In the Southern colonies, whites identified Africans ethnically when they arrived and seldom later . . . Jamaicans--who alone referred to slaves

by their country of origins long after they were unloaded and
sold--sprinkled tribal designations throughout their plantation records."
(22-23, 25) According to Mullin, these designations, which were a
practical tool for the Europeans in stereotyping Africans, allowed the
Africans to claim national connections and locate others of the same
group: "in an 1807 list from Westmoreland Parish, Jamaica, slaves
numbered 44 and 45, both named Peter, were then distinguished as Banda
and Ibo: three Fannys were Creole, Ibo, and Congo . . . Jamaicans knew
a great deal about shipmates, countrymen, and the 'New Negroes' first
reaction . . . . Advertisers wrote for a public able to depect Africans by
reference to norms or stereotypes of national characteristics: 'look more
like Eboe than a Coamantee': and 'Chambra but may be taken as a
Coramante'." 26-28.

12. One ritual that is based on the deification of ancestors is called
Nija. This word means "the way" in Kiswahilia. Milefi Kete Asante talks
about the celebration of Nija as part of the spectrum of critical pan-African
thought: "Nija is not the product of one or two minds, but the cumulative
experience of African People, expressed concretely in the lives of a small
segment. It is found among African-Americans but also exists in several
African countries.... A practice of Nija and the *Teachings of Nija*
constitutes the beginning of reconstruction. People who come to Nija have
usually passed through a redefinition phase." *Afrocentricity* (Trenton, NJ:
Africa World Press, 1991), 22-23.

13. G. Thomas Couser, "Oppression and Repression: Personal and
Collective Memory in Paule Marshall's *Praisesong for the Widow* and
Leslie Marmon Silko's *Ceremony*," in *Memory and Cultural Politics:
New Approaches to American Ethnic Literature*, eds. Amritjit Singh,
Joseph T. Skerrett Jr., and Robert E. Hogan (Boston: Northeastern
University Press, 1996), 106-120. Couser discusses the aspects of the
slave ship remembered as a crucial part of African American history and
the hallucinatory experience as a component of personal and racial
memories.

14. Athena Vrettos, "Curative Domains: Women, Healing and
History in Black Women's Narratives," *Women's Studies*, Vol. 16, no.
3-4, October 1989, 455-473.

15. "Followers of the traditional system [health practices passed
down from one generation to another among African American
healers/doctors] view the human being as an integration of body, mind
and spirit, all three of which must be properly cared for if it is to be
maintained. The body must be properly cared for if it is to function
normally: cleansed inside and out; kept warm; properly fed; appropriately
exercised; adequately rested. Health is not merely the absence of disease;
to elderly Sea Islands people it means the ability to live independently and
meet their own needs." Snow, *Walkin over Medicine*, 69, 73.

16. Abena P. Busia, "What Is Your Nation?: Reconnecting Africa and Her Diaspora Through Paule Marshall's *Praisesong for the Widow*," *Changing Our Own Words: Essays on Criticism, Theory and Writing by Black Women*, ed. Cheryl A. Wall (New Brunswick: Rutgers University Press, 1991), 211.

17. Carole Boyce Davies, "Mothering and Healing in Recent Black Women's Fiction," *Sage* Vol. 2.1 (1985), 41.

18. Angelita Reyes, "Carnival as an Archaelogical Site for Memory," *Memory, Narrative, and Identity: New Esssays in Ethnic American Literatures*, eds. Amritjit Singh, Joseph T. Skerrett Jr., and Robert E. Hogan (Boston: Northeastern University Press, 1994), 191.

19. Abena P. Busia, "What Is Your Nation?", 198.

BIBLIOGRAPHY

Books

Abrahams, Roger D., ed. *Afro-American Folktales: Stories from Black Traditions in the New World*. New York: Pantheon Books, 1985.

Angelou, Maya. *And Still I Rise*. New York: Random House, 1978.

Asante, Molefi Kete. *Afrocentricity*. Trenton, NJ: Africa World Press, Inc., 1991.

Bacher, Kenneth, et al., eds. *The New International Version Study Bible*. Grand Rapids, MI: Zondervan, 1985.

Beckley, Bruce R. *Joel Chandler Harris*. Athens: University of Georgia Press, 1987.

Bennett, Lerone, Jr. *Before the Mayflower: A History of Black America*. 5th Edition. New York: Penguin Books, 1982.

Bernhard, Virginia, Betty Brandon, Elizabeth Fox-Genovese, and Theda Perdue, eds. *Southern Women: Histories and Identities*. Columbia: University of Missouri Press, 1992.

Bogle, Donald. *Brown Sugar: Eighty Years of America's Black Female Superstars*. New York: Da Capo Press, 1990.

Bond, Horrace Mann. *Black American Scholars: A Study of Their Beginnings*. Detroit: Balamp, 1972.

Braxton, Joanne M. *Black Women Writing Autobiography: A Tradition Within a Tradition*. Philadelphia: Temple University Press, 1989.

Bush, Barbara. *Slave Women in Caribbean Society, 1650-1838*. Bloomington: University of Indiana Press, 1990.

Carby, Hazel V. *Reconstructing Womanhood: The Emergence of the Afro-American Woman Novelist*. New York: Oxford University Press, 1987.

Christian, Barbara. *Black Feminist Criticism: Perspectives on Black Women Writers*. New York: Pergamon Press, 1985.

Collins, Patricia Hill. *Black Feminist Thought*. New York: Routledge, 1990.

Davies, Carole Boyce, and Elaine Savory Fido, eds. *Out of Kumbla: Caribbean Women and Literature.* Trenton, NJ: Africa World Press, Inc., 1994.

Davis, Charles T., and Henry Louis Gates Jr., eds. *The Slave's Narrative.* New York: Oxford University Press, 1985.

Deats, Sara Munson, and Lagretta Tallent Lenker, eds. *The Aching Hearth: Family Violence in Life and Literature.* New York: Plenum Press, 1991.

De Weever, Jacqueline. *Mythmaking and Metaphor in Black Women's Fiction.* New York: St. Martin's Press, 1991.

DuBois, W.E.B. *Darkwater: Voice From Within the Veil.* New York: Schocken Books, 1969.

Equiano, Olaudah or Gustavus Vassa the African. *Equiano's Travels.* Portsmouth: Heinemann Press, 1969.

Escott, Paul D., and David R. Goldfield. *Major Problems in the History of the American South, Volume I: The Old South.* Lexington: D.C. Heath Publications, 1990.

Evans, Mari. ed. *Black Women Writers (1950-1980): A Critical Evaluation.* New York: Anchor Books, 1984.

Fabre, Geneviève, and Robert O'Meally. *History and Memory in African-American Culture.* New York: Oxford University Press, 1994.

Feder, Lillian. *Madness in Literature.* Princeton: Princeton University Press, 1980.

Fehrenbacher, Don E. *Slavery, Law, and Politics: The Dred Scott Case in Historical Perspective.* New York: Oxford University Press, 1981.

Feldstein, Stanley. *Once a Slave: The Slave's View of Slavery.* New York: William Morrow, 1970.

Foucault, Michel. *Madness and Civilization: A History of Insanity in the Age of Reason.* New York: Pantheon Books, 1965.

Franklin, John Hope, and Alfred A. Moss Jr., eds. *From Slavery to Freedom.* New York: McGraw-Hill, 1988.

Gates, Henry Louis, Jr. *Figures in Black: Words, Signs, and the "Racial" Self.* New York: Oxford University Press, 1987.

Genovese, Eugene D. *Roll, Jordan, Roll: The World the Slaves Made.* New York: Vintage Books, 1976.

Giddings, Paula. *When and Where I Enter: The Impact of Black Women on Race and Gender in America.* New York: Bantam Books, 1988.

Grier, William H., and Prince M. Cobb. *Black Rage.* New York: Bantam Books, 1968.

Gutmann, Herbert G. *Who Built America?: Working People and The Nation's Economy, Politics, Culture and Society.* New York: Pantheon Books, 1989.

-----*The Black Family in Slavery and Freedom 1750-1925*. New York: Pantheon Books, 1976.

Gwin, Minrose C. *Black and White Women of the Old South*. Knoxville: University of Tennessee Press, 1985.

Harris, Middleton, Morris Levitt, Roger Furman, and Ernest Smith, eds. *The Black Book*. New York: Random House 1974.

Hegel, G.W.F. *The Philosophy of History*. New York: Dover Publications, 1956.

Hernton, Calvin C. *The Sexual Mountain and Black Women Writers*. New York: Doubleday, 1987.

-----*Sex and Racism in America*. New York: Anchor Books, 1988.

Higman, Barry. *Slave Population and Economy in Jamaica 1807-1834*. New York: Cambridge University Press, 1976.

Hite, Molly. *The Other Side of the Story: Structures and Strategies of Contemporary Feminist Narratives*. Ithaca: Cornell University Press, 1989.

hooks, bell. *Outlaw Culture: Resisting Representations*. New York: Routledge, 1994.

-----*Talking Back: Thinking Feminist—Thinking Black*. Boston: South End Press, 1989.

Horton, Mary Beth. *Major Problems in American Women's History*. Lexington: D.C. Heath Company, 1989.

Houston, Lawrence N. *Psychological Principles and the Black Experience*. New York: University Press of America, 1990.

Howard, Lillie P. *Alice Walker and Zora Neale Hurston: The Common Bond*. Westport, CT: Greenwood Press, 1993.

Hull, Gloria T. *Color, Sex, and Poetry: Three Women Writers of the Harlem Renaissance*. Bloomington: Indiana University Press, 1987.

Hurston, Zora Neale. *Their Eyes Were Watching God*. New York: Harper & Row Publishing, 1990 (1937).

Jacobs, Harriet, *Incidents in the Life of a Slave Girl Written by Herself*. Ed. Jean Fagan Yellin. Cambridge: Harvard University Press, 1987.

Jones, Jacqueline. *Labor of Love, Labor of Sorrow: Black Women, Work, and the Family from Slavery to the Present*. New York: Vintage Books, 1995.

Judy, Ronald A. T. *Dis-Forming the American Canon: African-Arabic Slave Narratives and the Vernacular*. Minneapolis: University of Minnesota Press, 1993.

Karolides, Nicholas J., Lee Burress, and John M. Kean, eds. *Censored Books: Critical Viewpoints*. Metuchen, NJ: The Scarecrow Press, Inc., 1993.

Levi-Strauss, Claude. *The Savage Mind.* Chicago: University of Chicago Press, 1966.

Majors, Monroe A. *Noted Negro Women: Their Triumphs and Activities.* New York: Books for Libraries Press, 1971.

Marshall, Paule. *Praisesong for the Widow.* New York: E.P. Dutton Inc., 1984.

McDowell, Deborah E. *The Changing Same: Black Women's Literature, Criticism, and Theory.* Bloomington: Indiana University Press, 1995.

Meiring, Jane. *Thomas Pringle: His Life and Times.* Capetown: A.A. Balkema, 1968.

Mintz, Sidney W. *Caribbean Transformations.* Chicago: Aldine Press, 1974.

Morrison, Toni. *Beloved.* New York: Penguin Books, 1988.

Mullin, Michael. *Africa in America: Slave Acculturation and Resistance in the American South and the British Caribbean 1736-1831.* Chicago: University of Illinois Press, 1994.

Nash, Gary B. *Red, White, and Black: The Peoples of Early North America.* Englewood Cliffs: Prentice Hall Publications, 1992.

Paulme, Denise, ed. *Women in Tropical Africa.* Berkeley: University of California Press, 1963.

Poussaint, Alvin. *Why Blacks Kill Blacks.* New York: Emerson Hall, 1972.

Prince, Mary. *The History of Mary Prince, A West Indian Slave, Related by Herself.* Ed. Moira Ferguson. Ann Arbor: University of Michigan Press, 1993.

Pryse, Marjorie, and Hortense J. Spillers. *Conjuring: Black Women, Fiction, and Literary Tradition.* Bloomington: Indiana University Press, 1985.

Romano, Nicolas. *Women of Africa: Roots of Oppression.* Trans. Maria Rosa Cutrufelli. London: Zed Press, 1983.

Russell, Kathy, Midge Wilson, and Ronald Hall, eds. *The Color Complex: The Politics of Skin Color Among African Americans.* New York: Anchor Books, 1992.

Russell, Sandi. *Render Me My Song: African-American Women Writers from Slavery to the Present.* New York: St. Martin's Press, 1990.

Singh, Amritjit, Joseph T. Skerrett, Jr., and Robert E. Hogan, eds. *Memory and Cultural Politics: New Approaches to American Ethnic Literature.* Boston: Northeastern University, 1996.

Smith, Valerie, Lea Baechler, and A. Walton Litz. eds. *African American Writers: Profiles of Their Lives and Works from the 1700's to the Present.* New York: Collier Books, 1993.

Smitherman, Geneva. *Talkin and Testifyin: The Language of Black America.* Detroit: Wayne State University, 1977.

Snow, Loudell F. *Walkin over Medicine*. Boulder: Westview Press, 1993.

Spivak, Gayatri. *In Other Words: Essays in Cultural Politics*. New York: Routledge, 1988.

Tate, Claudia. *Black Women Writers at Work*. New York: Continuum, 1983.

Terborg-Penn, Rosalyn, Sharon Harley, and Andrea Benton Rushing, eds. *Women in Africa and the African Diaspora*. Washington, D.C.: Howard University Press, 1987.

Walker, Alice. *In Search of Our Mother's Gardens: Womanist Prose*. New York: Harcourt Brace Jovanovich, 1983.

-----*The Color Purple*. New York: Pocket Books, 1982.

Wall, Cheryl. *Changing Our Own Words: Essays on Criticism, Theory and Writing by Black Women*. New Brunswick: Rutgers University Press, 1991.

Wallace, Michele. *Invisibility Blues: From Pop to Theory*. New York: Verso, 1990.

-----*Black Macho and the Myth of the Superwoman*. New York: Verso, 1990.

Washington, Mary Helen. *Invented Lives: Narratives of Black Women 1860-1960*. New York: Anchor Press, 1987.

White, Deborah Gray. *Arn't I A Woman: Female Slaves in the Plantation South*. New York: Norton Press, 1985.

Williams, Chancellor, *The Destruction of Black Civilization*. Chicago: Third World Press, 1987.

Williams, Eric. *Capitalism and Slavery*. Chapel Hill: University of North Carolina Press, 1994.

Willis, Susan. *Specifying: Black Women Writing the American Experience*. Madison: University of Wisconsin Press, 1987.

Winchell, Donna Haisty. *Alice Walker*. New York: Twayne Publishers, 1992.

Winter, Kari J. *Subjects of Slavery, Agents of Change: Women and Power in Gothic Novels and Slave Narratives, 1790-1865*. Athens: The University of Georgia Press, 1992.

Wintz, Cary D. *Black Culture and the Harlem Renaissance*. Houston: Rice University Press, 1988.

Wisk, Gina. *Black Women's Writing*. New York: St. Martin's Press, 1993.

Articles and Essays

Berrian, Brenda F. "Claiming An Identity: Caribbean Women Writers in English." *Journal of Black Studies*. 25.2 December 1994, 200-16.

Busia, Abena P. A. "What Is Your Nation?: Reconnecting Africa and Her Diaspora through Paule Marshall's *Praisesong for the Widow*." In *Changing Our Own Words: Essays on Criticism, Theory and Writing by Black Women*, ed. Cheryl Wall. New Brunswick: Rutgers University Press, 1991, 196-212.

Carby, Hazel. "In the Quiet, Undisputed Dignity of My Womanhood." In *Reconstructing Womanhood: The Emergence of the Afro-American Woman Novelist*. New York: Oxford University Press, 1987, 94-120.

Christian, Barbara. "Trajectories of Self-Definition." In *Conjuring: Black Women, Fiction, and Literary Traditions*, ed. Marjorie Pryse and Hortense J. Spillers. Bloomington: Indiana Press, 1985, 231-48.

-----"But What Do We Think We're Doing Anyway: The State of Black Feminist Criticism(s) or My Version of a Little Bit of History." In *Changing Our Own Words: Essays on Criticism, Theory, and Writing by Black Women*, ed. Cheryl Wall. New Brunswick: Rutgers University Press, 1991, 58-84.

-----"Alice Walker: The Black Woman Artist as Wayward." In *Black Feminist Criticism: Perspective on Black Women Writers*. New York: Pergamon Press, 1985, 81-102.

Couser, G. Thomas. "Oppression and Repression: Personal and Collective Memory in Paule Marshall's *Praisesong for the Widow* and Leslie Marmon Silko's *Ceremony*." In *Memory and Cultural Politics: New Approaches to American Ethnic Literatures*, ed. Amritjit Singh, Joseph T. Skerrett Jr., and Robert E. Hogan. Boston: Northeastern University Press, 1996, 106-120.

Cudjoe, Selwyn R. "Maya Angelou: The Autobiographical Statement Updated." In *Reading Black, Reading Feminist*, ed. Henry Louis Gates, Jr. New York: Meridian Books, 1990, 272-306.

Davies, Carole Boyce. "Writing Home: Gender and Heritage in the Works of Afro-Caribbean/American Women Writers." In *Out of the Kumbla: Caribbean Women and Literature*, eds. Carole Boyce Davies and Elaine Savory Fido. Trenton, NJ: Africa World Press Inc., 1994, 59-74.

Davies, Carole Boyce. "Mothering and Healing in Recent Black Women's Fiction." *Sage*. Vol 2.1, 1985, 41-43.

Davis, Angela. "Reflections on the Black Woman's Role in the Community of Slaves." *Black Scholar*. Vol.3, No.4, December 1971, 3-15.

Dill, Bonnie Thornton. "Race, Class, and Gender: Prospects For an All-Inclusive Sisterhood." *Feminist Studies*. Vol.9, no.1, Spring 1983, 131-150.

Dixon, Melvin. "Between Memory and History: *Les Lieux de Mémoire*." *Representations* 26, Spring 1989, 7-24.

Dixon, Melvin. "The Black Writer's Use of Memory." In *History and Memory in African American Culture*, eds. Fabre and O'Meally. New York: Oxford University Press, 1994, 18-27.

Fanin, Alice. "The Pattern for Psychic Survival in *Their Eyes Were Watching God* and *The Color Purple*." In *Alice Walker and Zora Neale Hurston: The Common Bond*, ed. Lillie P. Howard. Westport: Greenwood Press, 1993, 45-56.

Gaspar, Barry D. "The Antigua Slave Conspiracy of 1736." *William and Mary Quarterly* 35:2, April 1978, 308-323.

Gilroy, Paul. "Living Memory," an interview with Toni Morrison. In *City Limits Magazine* (London) 31 March – 7 April 1988.

Harrison, James. "Negro English" *Anglia III*. (1884).

Henderson, Mae Gwendolyn. "Speaking in Tongues: Dialogics, Dialectics, and the Black Woman Writer's Literary Tradition." In *Changing Our Own Words: Essays on Criticism, Theory, and Writing by Black Women*, ed. Cheryl Wall. New Brunswick: Rutgers University Press, 1989, 16-37.

Hirsh, Marianne. "Maternal Narratives: Cruel Enough to Stop the Blood." In *Toni Morrison: Critical Perspectives Past and Present*, eds. Henry Louis Gates, Jr. and K.A. Appiah. New York: Amistad, 1993, 261-273.

Holloway, Karla F. C. "Revision and (Re)membrance." *Black American Literature Forum*. Vol. 24, no. 4, Winter 1990, 617-631.

hooks, bell. "Reading and Resistance." In *Alice Walker: Critical Perspectives Past and Present*, ed. Henry Louis Gates, Jr. and K. A. Appiah. New York: Amistad, 1993, 284-95.

Hull, Gloria T. "The Black Woman Writer and the Diaspora." *The Black Scholar*. Vol.17, no.2, March/April 1986, 2-4.

"Is Skin Color Still a Problem in Black America?" *Ebony Magazine.* December 1984, 66-70.

Jamison-Hall, Angelene. "She's Just Too Womanish for Them: Alice Walker and *The Color Purple*." In *Censored Books: Critical Viewpoints*, eds. Nicholas J. Karolides, Lee Burress, and John M. Kean. Metuchen: The Scarecrow Press, Inc., 1993, 191-200.

Kopytoff, Barbara. "Jamaican Maroon Political Organization: The Effects of the Treaties." *Social and Economic Studies* 25, June 1976, 101-120.

Krumholz, Linda. "The Ghost of Slavery: History and Recovery in Toni Morrison's *Beloved*." *African American Review*. Vol.26, no.3, 1992, 395-408.

Leclair, Thomas. "The Language Must Not Sweat: A Conversation with Toni Morrison." In *Toni Morrison: Critical Perspectives, Past and Present*, eds, Henry Louis Gates, Jr. and K. A. Appiah. New York: Amistad, 1993, 369-377.

Morrison, Toni. "Rediscovering Black History." *New York Times Magazine*. 11 August 1974, 13-21.

-----"Rootedness: The Ancestor as Foundation." *Black Women Writers (1950-1980): A Critical Evaluation,*, ed. Mari Evans. New York: Doubleday, 1984, 339-345.

-----"What the Black Woman Thinks About Women's Lib," *New York Times Magazine* (22 August 1971), 63.

-----"Site of Memory," In *Investing the Truth: The Art and Craft of Memoir*, ed. William Zinsser. Boston: Houghton Mifflin Company, 1987, 101-124.

Naylor, Gloria, and Toni Morrison. "A Conversation." *The Southern Review*. Vol.21, No.3 , Summer 1985, 567-593.

O'Neale, Sondra. "Reconstruction of the Composite Self: New Images of Black Women in Maya Angelou's Continuing Autobiography" In *Black Women Writers (1950-1980): A Critical Evaluation*, ed. Mari Evans. New York: Anchor Books, 1984, 25-36.

Paquet, Sandra Pouchet. "The Heartbeat of a West Indian Slave: *The History of Mary Prince.*" *African American Review*. 26.1, Spring 1992, 131-146.

Pettis, Joyce. "Self Definition and Redefinition in Paule Marshall's *Praisesong for the Widow.*" In *Perspectives of Black Popular Culture*, ed. Harry B. Shaw. Bowling Green: Bowling Green State University Popular Press, 1990, 93- 100.

Philip, Marlene Nourbese. "The Absence of Writing or How I Almost Became a Spy." In *She Tries Her Tongue, Her Silence Softly Breaks*, ed. Marlene Nourbese Philip. East Haven, CT: Inbooks, 1995, 10-25.

Pryse, Marjorie. "Zora Neale Hurston, Alice Walker, and the 'Ancient Power' of Black Women." In *Conjuring: Black Women, Fiction, and Literary Traditions*, eds. Marjorie Pryse and Hortense J. Spillers. Bloomington: Indiana University Press, 1985. 1-23.

Rauch, Esther Nettles. "Paul Laurence Dunbar." In *African American Writers: Profiles of Their Lives and Works from the 1700s to the Present*. New York: Collier Books, 1993, 67-80.

Reyes, Angelita. "Carnival as an Archaeological Site for Memory." In *Memory, Narrative, and Identity: New Essays in Ethnic American Literatures*, eds. Amritjit Singh, Joseph T. Skerrett Jr., and Robert E. Hogan. Boston: Northeastern University Press, 1994, 179-97.

Rigney, Barbara Hill. "The Disremembered and Unaccounted For." In *Toni Morrison: Critical Perspectives, Past and Present*, eds. Henry Louis Gates, Jr. and K. A. Appiah. New York: Amistad, 1993, 62-73.

Rubenstein, Roberta. "Pariahs and Community." In *Toni Morrison: Critical Perspectives, Past and Present*, eds. Henry Louis Gates, Jr. and K. A. Appiah. New York: Amistad, 1993. 126- 155.

Spillers, Hortense. "A Hateful Passion, A Lost Love." In *Toni Morrison: Critical Perspectives, Past and Present*, eds. Henry Louis Gates, Jr. and K. A. Appiah. New York: Amistad, 1993, 210-235.

----- "Cross-Currents, Discontinuities: Black Women's Fiction." In *Conjuring: Black Women, Fiction, and Literary Tradition*, eds. Majorie Pryse and Hortense J. Spillers. Bloomington: Indiana University Press, 1985, 249-261.

Spivak, Gayatri. "Can the Subaltern Speak?" In *Marxism and the Interpretation of Culture*, eds. C. Nelson and L. Grossberg. Basingstoke, England: Macmillan Education, 1988, 271- 313.

Thicknesse, Philip. *Memoirs and Anedoctes of P. Thicknesse*, Two Volumes. London: Printed for the Author, 1788-91.

Thurman, Judith. "A House Divided." *The New Yorker*. 2 November 1987, 175.

Vrettos, Athena. "Curative Domains: Women, Healing and History in Black Women's Narratives." *Women's Studies*, Vol. 16. (1989), 455-73.

Wallace, Michele. "Blues for Mr. Spielberg." In *Invisibility Blues: From Pop to Theory*. New York: Verso, 1990, 67-76.

Waters-Dawson, Emma. "From Victim to Victor: Walker's Women in *The Color Purple.*" *The Aching Hearth: Family Violence in Life and Literature*, eds. Sara Munson Deats and Lagretta Tallent Lenker. New York: Plenum Press, 1991, 255-68.

Wilentz, Gay. "Towards a Spiritual Middle Passage Back: Paule Marshall's Diasporic Vision in *Praisesong for the Widow.*" *Obsidian II*. Vol 5, no. 3 , 1990, 1-21.

Williams, Delores S. "Black Women's Literature and The Task of Feminist Theology." In *Immaculate and Powerful: The Female in Sacred Image and Social Reality*, eds. Clarissa W. Atkinson, Constance H. Buchanan and Margaret R. Miles. Boston: Beacon Press, 1985, 88-110.

Archival Sources

Anti-Slavery Monthly Reporter 1825-1833. John Rylands University Library of Manchester, England, Anti-Slavery Collection.

Index

abolition, 75
abolitionist, 14, 16, 36, 41, 42
abort, 58, 59
abortions, 59
accommodation, 56, 57
Africa, 4, 5, 12, 20, 86, 87, 89, 96, 109
African American community, 14, 18
African American history, 5
African American missionaries, 87
African American tradition, 74
African American women, 6
African Americans, 5, 6, 7, 13, 14, 20, 21,
    22, 31, 55, 56, 57, 62, 73, 76, 87, 99,
    108, 110, 118, 119, 120
African ancestral traditions, 119
African ancestry, 110, 112
African Caribbean celebration, 118
African community, 62
African diaspora, 43, 118
African heritage, 23
African legacies, 4, 20, 110, 111, 113
African rituals, 117
African roots, 6
African traditions, 4, 12, 30, 110, 118
African women, 30, 43
African-inspired rituals, 119
African-inspired traditions, 119
African-rooted ancestral legacies, 3
Africanized Christian, 12
Africans, 3, 6, 7, 12, 13, 16, 17, 20, 22, 30,
    31, 33, 34, 43, 44, 87, 105, 110, 116
Afro-Caribbean Rituals, 105
Afro-Caribbean, 112
Afro-Caribbean/American women, 29
Afrocentric, 3, 6, 8, 15, 22
Alexander, Ziggy, 34
The American Baptist, 57
American South, 32
American dream, 106, 108, 113, 119, 120
ancestors, 67, 70, 71, 105, 114, 115, 117
ancestral, 76, 105
ancestral legacies, 83
ancestry, 62, 99
Angelou, Maya, 23
Anti-Slavery Monthly Report, 35

Antigua, 31, 33
Aunt Jemima, 17
autobiographies, 76
The Autobiography of an Ex-Colored
    Man, 91

baptism, 40, 41
Barbados, 31
Bassett, P.S., 8
The Beg Pardon, 116, 117
Beg Pardon dance, 116
bell hooks, 21
Beloved, 8, 9, 10, 11, 15, 18, 19, 55, 57,
    58, 59, 61, 63, 75, 76, 105
Bermuda, 37
biographies, 76
The Black Book, 57
Black Feminist Criticism, 88
Black No More, 91
"Black Women's Literature and the Task
    of Feminist Theology", 95
The Blacker the Berry (1929), 91
The Bluest Eye, 91
Bond, Horrace Mann, 88
Buchner, J.H., 41
Bush, Barbara, 32, 33
Busia, Abena P., 116, 118

Carby, Hazel, 21, 89
Caribbean slave narrative, 43
Caribbean slavery, 119
Caribbean, 4, 5, 12, 30, 31, 36, 111
"Carnival as an Archaeological Site for
    Memory," 118
Chesnutt, Charles, 90
children, 58, 59, 61, 87, 94
Christian mythology, 110
Christians, 16, 19, 42, 110, 111
Christian, Barbara, 21, 88, 108, 113
Christianity, 36, 110
Christianization, 4, 12
citizenship, 84, 86
Civil War, 84, 89
class, 6
Collins, Pat Hill, 15

colonization, 43
colonizers, 86
color, 69, 91, 97, 99
The Color Purple, 5, 12, 15, 16, 18, 19, 22,
    83, 84, 94, 95, 98, 99, 105
colors, 69
commodification, 61
community, 4, 5, 9, 10, 11, 12, 13, 14, 15,
    17, 19, 20, 21, 22, 23, 32, 33, 35, 39,
    43, 44, 55, 57, 58, 61, 62, 63, 65, 67,
    68, 70, 72, 73, 74, 76, 83, 84, 85, 86,
    87, 88, 89, 90, 92, 96, 98, 99, 105, 116
concubine, 18, 63
Cooper, Anna Julia, 89

Dahomey, 33
dark-skinned, 89, 91, 92
Davies, Carol Boyce, 29, 118
Davis, Angela, 57
de Weever, Jacqueline, 74
dialect, 7, 14, 16
Diaspora, 3, 6, 8, 10, 11, 13, 14, 17, 20, 21,
    23, 29, 30, 43, 44, 87, 88, 105, 113, 120
Diasporan, 10
diasporic, 17, 21, 22, 105, 120
disenfranchised, 84
disenfranchisement, 84
Dixon, Melvin, 11
Douglas, Betto, 35
Douglass, Frederick, 43
Du Bois, W.E.B., 5, 90

emancipated, 86
Emancipation, 4, 6, 14, 19, 55, 60, 89, 90
Emancipation Proclamation, 60
Equiano, Olaudah, 33, 43
Eurocentric, 12, 16
exploitation, 60, 63, 84, 89, 92, 106
exploited, 71

fable, 74
Fabre, Geneviève, 20, 21
fair-skinned, 89
Faulkner, 20
Fauset, Jessie, 7, 14, 91
female revolt, 9, 58
Ferguson, Moira, 39
Figures in Black, 13
folklore, 11

folktales, 10
Fourteenth Amendment, 60
freedom, 4, 5, 6, 12, 13, 14, 16, 35, 43, 60,
    61, 65, 66, 68, 69, 70, 72, 76, 86, 96
"Frustration and Adjustment," 56

Garner, Margaret, 5, 8, 9, 10, 57, 58, 59,
    62
Garvey, Marcus, 90
Gates, Henry Louis Jr., 10, 11, 13
gender, 89, 92, 98
genocide, 22, 56
Genovese, Eugene, 56, 57
ghosts, 11
Gilbert, Sarah, 39
Giles v. Harris (1903), 84
Giles v. Teasley (1904), 84
God, 69, 72, 73, 88, 95, 96, 97, 98, 99, 109
griot, 62

Harlem, 18, 106, 107
Harlem Renaissance, 7, 14
Harper, Frances Ellen Watkins, 90
Hegel, G.W.F., 10, 11
heritage, 12, 17, 107, 108, 110, 113, 116
Higman, Barry, 37
history, 3, 5, 6, 7, 8, 9, 10, 11, 12, 13, 20,
    21, 23, 31, 32, 63, 64, 69, 71, 75, 83,
    84, 99, 113, 118
*The History of Mary Prince, A West Indian
    Slave, Related by Herself*, 4, 13, 29, 32,
    34, 43
Houston, Lawrence N., 56
Hughes, Langston, 107
Hurston, Nora Zeale, 7, 14, 88
Hurston's vernacular, 14

Ibo Landing, 107, 108, 109, 112
Ibos, 12, 33, 119
identity, 3, 5, 6, 12, 16, 17, 18, 21, 23, 29,
    43, 44, 62, 76, 84, 86, 87, 88, 96, 105,
    106, 107, 108, 111, 112, 114, 120
image, 6, 13, 16, 17, 18, 19, 22, 23, 60, 61,
    66, 89, 96
image/identity, 3
imperialism, 16
incest, 88
Incidents in the Life of a Slave Girl, 29

infanticide, 8, 56, 57, 59, 62, 65, 66, 67, 69, 71, 72, 73
inferiority, 32
The Interesting Narrative of the Life of Olaudah Equiano, or Gustavus Vassa the African, 29
isolated, 83, 96, 105
isolation, 87, 88, 92, 94, 95, 112, 115, 120

Jacobs, Harriet, 43
Jamaica, 34
Jamaican Maroon, 33
Jamison-Hall, Angelene, 95
Jezebel, 17, 19
Johnson, James Weldon, 91
Jones, Jacqueline, 61

Krumholz, Linda, 75

Labor of Love, Labor of Sorrow, 61
language, 3, 13, 14, 15, 16, 21, 22, 23, 29, 38, 42, 74, 76
Larsen, Nella, 6, 91
legacies, 3, 9, 13, 16, 74, 89, 106, 110
legend, 12, 109, 118
Levi-Strauss, Claude, 7
light skin, 89, 90
light-skinned, 90
lighter skin, 90, 92
lighter skinned, 89
literary tradition, 21
Locke, Alain, 14
love, 9, 65, 68, 73, 76, 96, 97, 98, 99
lynchings, 84, 85

madness, 58, 65, 76, 86
manhood, 60
Maroon Wars, 33
Maroons, 30, 31, 33, 34
Marshall, Paule, 3, 5, 6, 7, 12, 14, 16, 105, 109, 113, 118, 119, 120
Mary Prince's narrative, 4, 8, 9
mask, 13, 113
masking, 13, 14
maternal narrative, 67
Maude Martha (1953), 91
memories, 55, 63, 65, 67, 105, 116
memory, 9, 10, 11, 12, 15, 20, 21, 22, 55, 61, 62, 74, 108, 109, 113, 116, 118

memory traditions, 18
message, 120
Methodist, 42
Methodist doctrines, 41
Methodist minister, 41
Middle Passage, 15, 64
missionaries, 87
morality, 89
Moravian Church, 40, 41
Moravian missionaries, 40
Moravian religion, 41
Moravianism, 40
Moravians, 41
Morrison, Toni, 3, 5, 6, 7, 8, 9, 10, 11, 14, 15, 20, 23, 55, 57, 58, 62, 66, 73, 74, 75, 91, 105
mother-daughter relationship, 65, 67
mulatto elite, 90
mulatto woman, 6
mulattoes, 90, 91
Mullin, Michael, 30
myth, 11, 74, 118
Mythmaking and Metaphor in Black Women's Fiction, 74
mythological, 108, 109
mythology, 74, 76

Nanny, 33
narrative, 4, 5, 6, 7, 11, 14, 15, 21, 29, 30, 32, 35, 36, 37, 39, 41, 42, 43, 44, 67, 76, 90, 106, 107, 109, 111, 118, 119
Narrative of the Life of Frederick Douglass, 29
Nora, Pierre, 11

obeah, 39
O'Meally, Robert, 20, 21
oral and personal histories, 76
oral historian, 62
oral histories, 62, 68, 73

Pan-African unity, 118
Pan-African, 118
Pariahs and Community, 56
Passing, 91
paternalism, 87
patriarchal, 89
Plessy v. Ferguson (1896), 84
Plum Bun, 91

Port Royal Jamaica, 34
post-Civil War, 55
post-Civil War America, 84
post-World War II, 5
praisesong, 118, 120
Praisesong for the Widow, 5, 12, 16, 18, 19, 105, 106
pregnancies, 59
prejudices, 56
Prince, Mary, 3, 4, 5, 6, 7, 8, 11, 14, 16, 19, 20, 30, 31, 43, 105
Pringle, Thomas, 5, 32, 36, 42
The Pringles, 41

Quicksand, 91
"In the Quiet Undisputed Dignity of My Womanhood," 89
quilting, 7, 93
quilts, 92, 93

race, 89, 92
race and gender, 89
race, class and gender, 7, 21
racism, 10, 15, 16, 20, 21, 85, 88, 94, 97, 106, 107, 119
racist, 108
rage, 113, 114, 120
rape, 60, 71, 84, 89
raped, 71
Reconstruction, 4, 5, 60, 84
recovery, 75
"Reflections on the Black Woman's Role in the Community of Slaves," 57
religion, 39, 72
rememories, 62, 63, 65, 67, 71, 72, 73
rememory, 8, 62, 63, 64, 65, 67, 70, 71, 73, 74, 76, 105
revolt, 9
Reyes, Angelita, 118
Rigney, Barbara Hill, 75
ringshout, 12, 109, 110, 111, 115, 117
rites, 105
rituals, 9, 12, 18, 105, 107, 109, 110, 114, 115, 116, 117, 119, 120
Roll, Jordan, Roll, 56
Rubenstein, Roberta, 56

Sapphire, 17
Schuyler, George, 91

segregation, 83, 84, 86, 90, 91
sexism, 16, 88, 94
sexuality, 39, 63, 89
She's Just Too Womanish for Them: Alice Walker and 'The Color Purple', 95
skin, 89, 97
skin color, 88, 90, 91, 92
skin tone, 89, 90
slave community, 62
slave narrative, 5, 8, 13, 14, 22, 29
slave narrator, 16
Slave Population and Economy in Jamaica (1807-1834), 37
Slave Women in Caribbean Society 1650-1838, 32
slavery, 4, 6, 7, 8, 9, 10, 13, 19, 20, 22, 32, 36, 37, 42, 43, 44, 55, 56, 57, 58, 59, 60, 61, 63, 65, 66, 67, 68, 69, 70, 71, 72, 73, 74, 75, 76, 86, 88, 89, 90, 107, 109, 119, 120
slavery's legacy, 14
Smitherman, Geneva, 13
soul, 61
South, 84
Spillers, Hortense, 21
spirituals, 13
Spivak, Gayatri, 21
stereotypes, 5, 6, 8, 14, 17, 18, 19, 20, 83, 99
stereotyping, 6
subjugation, 4, 8, 9, 13, 14, 23, 43, 73, 85, 88, 92, 98
Superwoman, 17

There is Confusion, 91
Thicknesse, Philip, 33
Thurman, Wallace, 91
Toussaint L'Ouverture, 4, 31
traditions, 9, 12, 32, 43, 105, 106, 110, 114, 115, 117, 119, 120
"Trajectories of Self-Definition," 113
Trinidad, 34

vernacular, 14
victimization, 12, 90, 95

Walker, Alice, 3, 5, 6, 7, 11, 14, 15, 19, 84, 85, 86, 87, 88, 89, 90, 91, 92, 93, 98, 105
Wallace, Michele, 86

warriors, 33
Washington, Booker T., 90
Wells, Ida B., 89
West Indies, 32
"What Is Your Nation?", 116
white historians, 6
Wilberforce, William, of the House of
    Lords, 32
Wilentz, Gay, 112
Williams v. Mississippi (1898), 84
Williams, Delores S., 95
Winchell, Donna H., 97
Winter, Kari J., 22
womanhood, 63, 87, 94
women warriors, 4

Yoruba, 33